Praise for *Where Cooking Begins*

"Carla Lalli Music knows the key ingredient in good cooking is enthusiasm. One of the things she does brilliantly in *Where Cooking Begins* is show you how to cultivate it. I love the way her savvy shopping know-how, streamlined sourcing tips, organizational smarts, and approachable recipes all come together in a single go-to volume. Most important? It's a book that triggers that 'let's cook that right now' feeling!"

—Heidi Swanson, author, *Super Natural Cooking*

"*Where Cooking Begins* is that rare book that truly makes you cook with confidence. With ninja skills, humor, and zero B.S., Carla nails it on every page, instilling lessons that your hands—and heart—will remember forever."

—Christine Muhlke, contributing editor, *Bon Appétit*

"Carla is the rare talent who combines a chef's sensibility with the mind-set of a busy mom—which means when it comes to dinner, simplicity is *everything*. Her flavor-packed meals, accompanied by no-nonsense guidance, will make you swoon. Keep this book next to your stove!"

—Maria Speck, author, *Simply Ancient Grains* and *Ancient Grains for Modern Meals*

"*Where Cooking Begins* is like having an amazing cook for a best friend who lets you follow her around the kitchen all day. Carla is that friend. She speaks to you in simple terms, she shows you techniques that apply to not just one recipe but several—all delicious. She shows you how to walk right up to your fridge without fear and make a meal to impress family and friends. Her book is perfect for the novice, but you would also find it on the 'favorites' shelf of any accomplished home cook. Upon my first read, I started cooking immediately."

—Jenni Konner, writer, producer, director, *Girls* and *Camping*

"This book is the next best thing to getting to hang out and cook with Carla. I've been a fan forever and have been waiting for this book."

—Andrew Tarlow, coauthor, *Dinner at the Long Table*

"Carla has a way with cooking that's relaxing, approachable, and delicious. That style shines throughout the pages of her gorgeous cookbook. From how to stock a pantry to her six essential cooking methods to her brilliant suggestions for ingredient swaps that make everyday dishes adaptable with what you have on hand or simply what you love, *Where Cooking Begins* is the ultimate kitchen cookbook."

—Tieghan Gerard, author, *Half Baked Harvest Cookbook*

[...] has found [...] to impart a failsafe formula for uncomplicated, adaptable, and delicious home cooking—the kind that lets you actually enjoy what you've cooked in the company of your friends and family at the table. No small feat! I've no doubt that *Where Cooking Begins* will become a dog-eared go-to in my kitchen."

—Danny Meyer, CEO, Union Square Hospitality Group; founder, Shake Shack; and author, *Setting the Table*

"Yes, Carla Lalli Music is *Bon Appétit*'s food director, but she's also a working mother who understands the real-life demands of shopping and cooking for a family. Thanks to both of those roles, she serves up recipes you not only *want* to make but *can* make."

—Adam Rapoport, editor in chief, *Bon Appétit*

"Carla's strikingly easygoing approach to cooking techniques in *Where Cooking Begins* allows every type of cook to learn something new. It's a must-have."

—Ignacio Mattos, coauthor, *Estela*

Where Cooking Begins

Where Cooking Begins

———

*Uncomplicated Recipes to
Make You a Great Cook*

———

Carla Lalli Music

Clarkson Potter/Publishers
New York

For my beautiful mother, Carole Lalli, who
showed me that love is a thing you can taste

Introduction: How I Cook at Home   9

Part 1: The Strategy
Cooking Begins Here

I've Had a Lot of Lives as a Cook   17

The Case for Small-Batch Cooking   18

A New Way to Shop   21

The Zoned-Out Kitchen   23

Pared-Down Pots, Pans, and Appliances   26

How to Live Forever on Fewer Spices   27

Spin It to Win It   31

Part 2: The Techniques
Salt and Pepper Cooking

Sauté   39

Pan-Roast   45

Steam   51

Boil and Simmer   57

Confit   63

Slow-Roast   69

Pastry Dough   75

Part 3: The Recipes
Cook with Abandon

Starring Produce   83

Egg-centric   115

Pasta and Grains   133

Chicken Lots of Ways, and a Duck   161

Fishes and Other Sea Creatures   181

Main Meats   195

Sunday Soups and Brothy Beans   223

Basic Baker's Sweets   239

Acknowledgments   266

Index   268

Introduction
How I Cook at Home

This is my perfect day: It's June, and a Saturday, the best day of the week by far. It's not too hot to sleep with the windows open but warm enough to kick off the covers when I wake up, take stock of the sun already pretty high up there, and realize with a spoonful of urgency that this day is not for wasting.

Saturday is farmers' market day in Fort Greene, my Brooklyn neighborhood, and I want to be there ahead of the crowds as much as I want to snag a primo spot at the beach before the parking lot fills up. The thoughts rush in—*What am I missing at the market right now while I'm lying in bed and the families with toddlers who've been up since 5 a.m. are going to buy because they got there before me?* My primary motivators are activated: anxiety, competition, and desire. What if there were sugar snap peas an hour ago, but there are none now? What if the best berries have already been scooped up? What if the parade of parents pushing strollers, couples walking dogs, and those people shepherding both strollers *and* dogs prevents me from getting a front-row spot to assess the lettuces? What if I am barred from one of life's greatest pleasures—blueberries that have never been refrigerated—because I arrive too late?

Some of my favorite recipes in this book came about on Saturdays like this one, when I had no plan for what I was going to cook but knew that whatever it was, it would all start with the farmers' market shop. There have been countless weekends when there was so much good stuff there that I struggled to carry all of it the two and a half blocks home, leafy greens sticking out of my totes and tickling the back of my neck, which is honestly a terrible sensation when you're trying to hang on to heavy bags. It's worth it, though, and I've eaten many juicy freestone peaches over the kitchen sink as reward for my stamina. I can think of numerous excursions at different times of the year when I was already overloaded but couldn't bear to leave without that giant squash/enormous watermelon/flat of tomatoes and called in family reinforcements to meet me halfway. I've eaten sautéed greens for breakfast because the bunches of Swiss chard were too big to fit in the fridge (Poached Egg and Silky Braised Greens, page 122) or spun the oven dial to a roasting temperature before unpacking so I could simply dispatch the squash I bought instead of parking it on my counter (Grains and Roasted Squash with Spicy Buttermilk Dressing, page 152), entered into a monogamous relationship with a single pastry dough that can be folded around any type of fruit, year-round, and become "a galette person," a classic marketer's spin designed to obscure the fact that my pie-crimping skills are crap (10-Minute Pastry Dough, page 241).

I'm a creature of habit and very stubborn, and I stuck to this market routine for years, motivated by berry-hoarder's greed alone. Shop, cook, eat, repeat. I've now realized that the hunt for peak ingredients is the way I shop for meal ideas, because I can see from the start where I want things to go. When something looks good—vibrant, colorful, abundant, or in fleeting supply—I cycle through a short list of universal cooking techniques in my arsenal and imagine how each one could transform what I'm looking at. (The six methods I rely on the most can be found in a step-by-step technique section that starts on page 33.) Ingredient + method = a rapid-fire run-through of all the things I could do with whatever I have the urge to buy, whether that means I'll pan-roast a thick steak or lazily simmer a pot of runner beans until their cooking liquid is good enough to drink. Over time I've come to realize that a direct line connects the special feelings I have about certain ingredients and the urgency with which I cook and eat them. Sometimes the abundance of peak produce inspires more dishes than there are hours in the day, and then the challenge is on me to consume everything I've bought before it starts to fade, since wasting what I've wrestled home is not an option. I'm okay with being excited by food shopping—it just means I cook what I buy. The upside of my occasional lack of restraint is that, over the years, I've figured out a lot of strategies for making great ingredients into meals and using everything up.

If you're at all like me, a day off and the farmers' market around the corner sounds like a great way to kick off a summer afternoon. But woman cannot live on local seasonal gems alone. There's an equally important, transactional, rational flip side to all my unstructured market outings, and it's called the internet.

I use online ordering regularly and strategically to keep my kitchen stocked with basics so I can come home at any hour of the day and put together a meal. The market has the fun stuff. But the internet's basics are my fundamental, functional items, and a mix of pantry and perishable— butter, eggs, milk and yogurt, lemons, condiments, oils, vinegars, nuts, spices, dried fruits, grains, canned tomatoes, beans, pasta, onions, and garlic. These ingredients may not increase my heart rate, but they're integral to most of my recipes. They're seasonless, so I can get them reliably year-round, and they're in heavy rotation; I replace and restock them frequently. They're essential and important, but not exactly special, which makes them perfect for outsourcing via an online grocery delivery service.

My hunting and gathering is split between these two approaches. When deciding what to shop for in person and what to order online, I give priority to quality-variable ingredients, and automate everything else. Here's how this plays out in practice: I'm motivated to visually inspect and smell-test the fresh scallops I'm planning to make for dinner, but I don't need to *personally* pick up the other necessities—kosher salt, some lemons, a bottle of olive oil. The romantic in me wants to shop strictly for ingredients that spark inspiration and the desire to cook, and my inner pragmatist knows that I can easily turn the food fantasy into reality if the building blocks are already in my kitchen, where I'll find them along with my cutting board, my pots and pans, and my knives when I get home.

As I write this, the traditional grocery store business is being upended by tech-enabled retailers, and there are more ways than ever for home cooks to find digital shopping options that make our lives easier. Relying on a combination of in-person market trips and online food shopping has saved me time, money, and hassle, and has removed the dread factor from grocery shopping. Online shopping is for everything heavy and bulky (four-pound bags of sugar, glass bottles of olive oil and vinegar, pounds of butter and pasta), plus all the things that come in cans (beans, coconut milk, whole peeled tomatoes). Instead of multihour weekend supermarket trips, I can place an order for groceries in twenty minutes. My hauls are lighter, my hours better spent. I stopped feeling guilty about paying a small premium to have someone else handle doorstep delivery a long time ago, and I'm simply grateful for the free time I get back in return.

Where Cooking Begins is a cookbook that makes shopping part of the recipes. If cooking and eating is a form of entertainment, shopping is the opening act. Linking these two moments—the going-and-getting and the coming-back-and-making—is what this book is all about. It will teach you a new way to shop that will inspire you to cook, and it is filled with no-fail techniques and textured recipes that will make you want to click on a burner and slide out a cutting board the minute you get home, because you can't wait to eat what you bought.

Part 1:
The Strategy
Cooking Begins Here

I've Had a Lot of Lives as a Cook

I grew up in a house with a mother who was (and is) an amazing cook, and I didn't start making my own meals until I left for college and realized that if I wanted to eat well, I needed to try to cook like she did.

I became a restaurant line cook in my twenties and made dishes that were beautiful and special but that no sane person would ever prepare at home. That's when I learned the mechanics of cooking and came to understand the direct relationship between the perfectness of an ingredient and the specialness of the finished dish.

I've spent the better part of a decade creating recipes and writing about food for *Bon Appétit* magazine and have been lucky enough to spend my days with passionate colleagues, working on how to share our obsessions with as many people as will listen.

But this book is about my life as a home cook. It's inspired by the meals I cook for my family and friends, the joy I take in feeding them, and it's filled with our favorite things to eat. It's also where I'm sharing my pared-back approach to shopping, planning, and meal-prepping for the first time. This very personal strategy for getting food into the house and then into our bellies has made me the happiest, most successful cook I've ever been, and in the pages that follow, I'll spell all that out for you.

If you get this far and skip ahead to the techniques, great. If you flip ahead even further and dive right into the recipes, I think that's awesome. If you look at the pretty pictures and give this book to a friend who you can convince to cook for you, bravo. And if you want to know where I'm going without having to do very much of anything, here it is in a nutshell:

Cooking begins when you feel the spark, when you know what you're hungry for.

Shop in person for the food that excites you. Shop small. Shop often.

Go online to get the ingredients that barely change with the seasons or that come in a box, bag, can, or jar.

Purchase only what you have room to store.

Cook what you buy; finish it up.

If you prefer a different flavor profile, change the recipe.

If you're missing something minor, leave it out.

If all else fails, there's always salt and pepper.

If you do all this, you'll make the food that you love and it will be delicious.
Still with me? Good. Let's cook.

The Case for Small-Batch Cooking

I don't believe in big-batch cooking, but that wasn't always the case.

My sons are big kids now, but a few years ago, when my firstborn was in grade school and his little brother was a toddler, my habit was to shop for groceries in big waves, cook a slew of meals over the weekend, and then make room for whole roasted chickens and quart containers of soups, stews, meatballs, and roasted vegetables in the fridge and freezer. This was done in an effort to stockpile meals and dole them out gradually until it was time for the next shopping trip. (On a more emotional level, I spent hours shopping and cooking on the weekends to try to lessen the guilt I felt about having kids and a career and not getting home in time to have dinner together during the week.) This well-intentioned strategy led instead to frustration about spending my downtime at the stove, and family-wide indifference about what was in the fridge. Sausage and bean soup is delicious for Sunday supper, but turns out to be a hard sell on Day Three. Inevitably and regrettably, uneaten food was thrown away.

It was the same thing over and over: I would plan for multiple meals, buy all the ingredients, and despite the bounty, food would go to waste. I was stuck in this cycle until a completely unplanned event forced me to abandon my supersized shopping and cooking habits.

The disruption came on suddenly, when my fifteen-year-old, 36-inch-wide refrigerator decided to stop making things cold, and it was time for a new one. I soon learned that we'd have to downsize to a 30-inch-wide model to fit into the same space (it's a boring tale about refrigerator door hinges). Long story short: I had no choice. We bought a new refrigerator and made plans for the switcheroo.

On New Refrigerator Eve, I had to remove every jar, squeeze bottle, and scrap of kale from the old fridge. With everything out on the counter, I took a long hard look at my seventeen different hot sauces (literally, seventeen), many-years-old mustards, murky pickled things, brown half-bunches of herbs, salami nubs and fuzzy cheese rinds, unidentifiable things in jars with rusted lids, and frostbitten mystery bricks from the freezer. Flavor boosters like miso, mustard, capers, anchovies, horseradish, mayonnaise, sesame oil, kimchi, ketchup, and *most* of the hot sauces earned a *permanent* spot, but everybody else was voted off the island. It wasn't easy, but I threw a lot of crap out.

This mandatory decluttering forced me to whittle down to only those things I would use. Emboldened, I went through the same process with my spice drawer and ended up with an all-star inventory. Coriander seeds, crushed red pepper, mustard seeds, cumin, fennel, peppercorns, smoked and hot paprika, flaky sea salt, and even MSG made the cut (check out the full list of my essential spices on page 27). The two-year-old jar of dried rosemary did not.

The smaller refrigerator arrived, and after putting the streamlined inventory away and swooning over the all-new-everything upgrade, I realized there were fewer deep corners for losing track of things, smaller crisper drawers that simply accommodated less, and for the first time in a long time, I could see everything in there. I'm pretty sure I took a picture.

Small Fridge Kitchen was the beginning of a new era of cooking and organization. I could finally admit to myself that I never enjoyed big-batch cooking. It felt like work, and it kept me from enjoying my time off on the weekends. Instead of a place to super-size everything, my kitchen became balanced among several categories that added up to the makings of a meal. I made sure I always had varied options: pantry items (grains, beans, canned tomatoes, dried noodles), produce that could hang out on the kitchen counter (like squash, avocados, sweet potatoes), a mix of delicate produce (herbs, salad greens, cucumbers) to use first, and hardy produce (broccoli, red cabbage, and carrots) that would last a little longer. Instead of being filled to the hilt with containers of homemade soups, stews, and braises, the freezer held nuts, homemade stock, cooked grains, bacon, leftover wine, butter, and Parmigiano rinds. With less available fridge space to work with, I started shopping smaller and more frequently, which—as it turns out—is the most efficient, least wasteful way to buy groceries.

I knew when we were running low on things because there was less of everything, and I took great pleasure in using things up (I had a debt of guilt for throwing those other things out). With grains, beans, multipurpose condiments, and good-looking produce always on hand, preparing a vegetarian meal was a no-brainer. "Put an egg on it?" was a menu add-on anyone could request. For a day-of dinner with a little more staying power (I live with three dudes, remember?), I'd buy a steak, some sausages, a nice piece of fish, or a pack of chicken thighs on the way home from work.

Small-scale cooking looks like this: Your kitchen is stocked with evergreen items across the board. On your way home in the evening, you stop off to pick up a nice fatty pork chop and a big bunch of mustard greens. You breeze through checkout (express lane, always) and spend the rest of your commute mentally planning your meal. You can draw on the ingredients and inventory waiting for you at home. You can sauté the greens with olive oil, some mustard seeds, and a drained can of white beans, then round that out with a knob of butter while the chop pan-roasts in a skillet on the next burner. Or, you can thinly slice the meat off the bone, cook it hot and fast, then deglaze the pan with red wine vinegar to make a warm, smoky vinaigrette to dress the washed and torn greens. You might pound out the chop, coat it with Dijon mustard and bread crumbs and broil it before topping it with a zingy slaw made with thinly sliced mustard greens and lots of fresh lemon juice. In each scenario, the chop and the greens carry the meal, but the already-stocked items at home provide flexibility, flavor, and options.

It's been years since I shopped with a recipe in hand or a concrete plan for the week ahead. Instead, I start roughing out a recipe in my imagination while I decide what to buy. If I come home with a lot of greens, I draw on my prestocked inventory to find a way to make them the center of my next meal. That could mean using the wheat berries in my pantry drawer to make a big grain bowl, or slowly cooking the greens down with olive oil and garlic, then adding them to a dozen-egg frittata (see recipe on page 117). As I reckon with the multiple quarts of carpe diem strawberries I bought, I will decide to make a compote, and because I already have cinnamon and star anise in my spice drawer, that's ample reason to add one of each. I apply the same thinking and methods when I shop for meat and fish, too. I might choose polenta to go with the chicken thighs I just brought home, then decide to braise the thighs with canned tomatoes because I like the idea of something saucy for that combo (Rosemary Chicken Ragu with Pressure Cooker Polenta, page 170). Each time, the shopping and cooking pattern is the same: I purchase a perishable and pair it with things from the stable of ingredients I keep at home.

It's not always peak growing season, and there are not always warm berries and heavy melons and squeaky corn to be had. There are many stretches of the year when there's no farmers' market to speak of, and the best ingredients come from afar (here on the East Coast, that's November to April, which is why I turn into such a freak come spring). But it doesn't matter where you shop, it matters *how* you shop. If you're excited and care about what you buy, you will waste less food. When you let go of the idea that you have to shop for a specific list of ingredients, you'll develop the confidence to wing it and make substitutions based on what you find in your own spice drawer. You will cook with all your senses and you will derive more pleasure from your meals. Simply put: This strategy will make you a better cook.

The realization that cooking begins before I've set foot in my kitchen is the inspiration for this book. Cooking begins with the idea of transforming something to make it taste better (like boiling a fava bean), or just for the purpose of enjoying it (putting salt on a cucumber). It begins when I decide what I want to bring home, and what someone else

should deliver. Cooking begins when I take stock of what's in the fridge and make a meal from what I find. (Before the fantasy gets out of control: Sometimes I stand at the kitchen counter and eat a bowl of cereal for dinner.) Letting a dish come together in my head, patching dinner together without relying on a meal plan, inviting friends over because I want to cook everything I've bought, and drawing on basic, functional ingredients that let me flex this way or that—that's the way I love to cook. I believe that anybody can shop, cook, and eat like this. That's why I wrote this cookbook, and I hope it changes your life as a cook, too.

A New Way to Shop

Shopping for food can make you want to cook, especially when the drudgery is minimized. There's *fun* food shopping, and *functional* food shopping. The key is knowing the difference, and exploiting it to your advantage.

You will spend less time in grocery stores and improve the overall quality of your food if you devote your attention to choosing ingredients wisely. Make in-person trips for things that make you hungry, the fun stuff—peak produce, excellent meat and sparkling fish, great dairy and bread. When you don't have a million things to get and you're not trying to keep track of a laundry list of needs on your phone, you'll end up picking out the things that truly appeal to you, and the choices you make will feel more special. You don't have to shop at a fancy purveyor or find a farmers' market to follow this advice. You just have to be open to flipping the script on the shopping trip.

How to shop for the fun stuff

Shop for food often and purchase only what you'll consume in the next couple of days. A perfect midweek shop may include a quick-cooking protein (chops, ground meat, or fish fillets, for example) and one or two vegetables to put into side dishes (maybe one cooked, one raw). On the weekend, try to shop early in the day so that if you want to marinate, slow-roast, or braise something, you have plenty of runway.

Focus on selecting quality-variable ingredients and make them the center of your meal. These are items that might look great, or not, and you should be there to assess and hand-select them. Think meat, poultry, seafood, and produce, and handmade products such as bread and cheese.

If you live near a farmers' market, visit it often. You don't even have to buy anything. Get familiar with the ups and downs of the seasons. Taste berries and snap peas from multiple stands and decide who's got the best ones. Ask the farmers what they're harvesting next.

At the grocery store, train yourself to examine, touch, and smell before you buy. It's hard to assess the fragrance and freshness of a bunch of herbs when it's encased in a plastic clamshell box, so choose whole ingredients over pre-packaged ones. Avoid precut fruits and vegetables, and vacuum-sealed seafood.

Shop small, waste less. Smaller hauls are less of a drag to get back home and take less time to put away. When I'm not at the farmers' market, I purposely shop without a shopping cart or basket to prevent impulse buys. When I can no longer free a finger to hook around the neck of a bottle and am using my chin to steady the pile of things balanced on my chest, it's time to check out. (This no-basket technique also prevents binge-buying at Sephora, just FYI.)

This approach to grocery shopping will remove logistical and psychological hurdles and set you up for success. Compare and contrast: I used to invite friends over for dinner and then plan very specific dishes to cook, cookbooks dog-eared and my laptop flipped open on the table in front of me. I love a list almost as much as I love crossing things out, so I'd write a detailed plan of what I wanted to serve and all the ingredients I needed to pull it off, neatly organized by section of the grocery store. But there was always that moment at the market when I would find that one of the things on my list was either missing or didn't look good (I specifically remember a lone bunch of radishes with droopy wet leaves and cracked, dried-out bulbs). Instead of crossing something off my list, I'd have to decide whether to proceed with a lousy vegetable, go to another store, or come up with another recipe on the fly.

That story sucks. I don't do that anymore. These days I still think through a mix of dishes and hash out a menu, but where in the past it would have said "shaved radish salad," now it says "crunchy veg thing." When I shop, I'll let the best vegetable for the job make itself known, and I am almost never disappointed. If you are picking out specific recipes before you go to the store, stop. If you find yourself buying things that don't look so hot but they were on your "list," and you end up pitching them into the garbage a few days later, quit it. Your meals should start with your fun shopping at the market and be executed with help from the functional ingredients at home. All of the recipes in this book are written to help you do that.

The functional categories

Any food that doesn't change much with the seasons (e.g., bananas), or comes in a jar, can, box, or sealed bag, is a functional ingredient. There are three categories of functional items: pantry items, spices and condiments, and seasonless perishables. These things might not be the sexiest in your kitchen, but you should feel a deep sense of attachment to them

nonetheless, since they provide both structure and variation every time you create a meal. Try ordering them online.

Fully functional food rules

Sign up for an online grocery delivery service such as Peapod, AmazonFresh, Google Shopping, or Fresh Direct. Many mainstream grocery chains across the United States now offer online shopping with same- or next-day delivery, including Whole Foods, Safeway, Kroger, Harris Teeter, and HyVee. I love going online to shop from independently owned specialty purveyors such as Penzey's, Kalustyan's, Zingerman's, Anson Mills, and Rancho Gordo, and they all will ship their exceptional products to you.

Keep a lean but diverse assortment of pantry items, seasonings, and perishables on hand. Your cupboards should be pared down, not stockpiled. There's no advantage to having more than one or two types of dried beans in the house. Same goes for whole grains and pasta—if you have a short, textured pasta shape plus a long strand, you're covered. Fewer things in the kitchen means less to keep track of, fewer items at risk of going stale or spoiling, and more available cabinet space.

Turnover should be high. Are there spices you bought years ago for a particular recipe that have been sitting dormant ever since? Have you had a bottle of vinegar for so long that it's not even got the current label and logo on it? We've all been there. Spend money on the things you reach for often, and use them up. If you've got dead stock on your hands, reassess and start fresh.

The Zoned-Out Kitchen

The size of your kitchen and the storage space you've been blessed with is less important than the way you set it up and keep it organized. The best advice I can give is to divide up your kitchen by category—or zone—just as every well-run restaurant kitchen I've ever worked in was set up. Even if you have a small kitchen with limited storage space, this will work: Designate distinct spaces as mini territories (see the lists on page 24). You'll always know where things are, or at least where they're supposed to be, and so will everyone else you live with. For example, keep all of your dried fruits in one area. If you're looking for dried apricots, but find only raisins, dates, and dried mangos in the usual spot, you can be fairly confident that the apricots aren't lurking somewhere else. No more tearing through every cabinet just to be sure.

Restaurant tricks for home cooks

Well-run restaurant kitchens know that a predictable physical layout makes things easy to find and minimizes food waste. These are the things I learned to do as a line cook that I've implemented at home ever since.

ABD: always be downsizing

Downsizing frees up space in the fridge, which makes your appliance run better, and also helps you keep track of what's running low. When the 32-ounce tub of yogurt is down to 1 cup, transfer it to a new jar. The quart of soup that is half consumed should be put back in a smaller container. Scrape the half-jar of jam into a smaller one. And save all those empty jars and lids!

Show some ID

I think of labeling as a banner ad that says "eat me." Salad dressings; leftovers; anything wrapped in foil; every bulk-bin grain that you're storing in a generic jar; every sauce, stock, or half of a steak that didn't get finished—label it all. If you don't know what something is, you will ignore it; food that's ignored ends up in the garbage. On the other hand, if you and everyone else in your household can easily identify a leftover, it will get eaten. All you need is a roll of masking tape and a Sharpie.

Finish before you start again

Anyone who has ever worked in a restaurant knows the FIFO rule: First in, first out. It's not rocket science. Finish the milk before you open a new quart. Don't buy carrots if you already have carrots. This will save you storage space, money, and annoyance. If you've discarded uneaten food (and considering that Americans throw away between 15 and 20 percent of the food they buy, you probably have), try to develop a genuine and practical intention to not repeat the misdeed.

Know your zones

Once you've divided your shopping trips between in-person mini-trips and online essentials, set up your kitchen to make it easy to put functional ingredients away, find them when you need them, and see when you need to restock. Coverage across the board gives you the ability to improv meals based on the fun ingredient you bring home and what you feel like eating. You don't necessarily need all of these items all of the time, but this is a useful, scannable list of things you can order online and have around, and the ideal places to store them.

Fridge

Bacon and/or pancetta

Butter

Cheese: Parmigiano, a melting cheese (mozzarella, cheddar), and feta

Citrus: lemons, limes, oranges

Condiments: mayonnaise, mustard, ketchup, hot sauce(s)

Eggs

Fresh chiles

Ginger

Jams and preserves

Maple syrup

Milk and buttermilk

Miso

Nut butter

Pickled things: capers, kimchi, prepared horseradish, olives, pickles

Smoked fish

Tahini

Yogurt and sour cream

Countertop

Black pepper

Cooking oils: ghee, coconut, and vegetable

Crushed red pepper (standard and/or Aleppo, gochugaru, Maras)

Garlic and onions

Mirin

Olive oil: everyday and finishing

Salt: kosher and flaky sea

Soy sauce

Vinegars: cider, red wine, white wine, unseasoned rice, and sherry

Freezer

Bread, bread crumbs
Cooked grains (rice and/or farro)
Chicken, beef, fish and/or pork bones for
    making stock
Frozen fruit
Ham hocks
Homemade stock
Homemade tomato sauce
Leftover red and white wine, for cooking
Nut, seed, and alt-flours (e.g., buckwheat flour,
    flaxseed meal)
Nuts: almonds, hazelnuts, walnuts
Parmigiano rinds
Sausages

Baking Supplies

Baking soda and baking powder
Chocolate bars, chocolate chips, and cocoa powder
Cooking spray
Cornstarch
Flour: all-purpose, cake, whole wheat
Gelatin and pectin
Honey
Molasses
Sprinkles, decorations, birthday candles
Sugar: granulated, brown, raw
Vanilla extract and vanilla beans

Dry Storage / Cans and Jars

Backup condiments
Canned beans
Canned whole tomatoes
Jarred or canned fish: tuna, anchovies, sardines
Unsweetened coconut milk

Dry Storage / Bags and Boxes

Dried beans
Dried fruits
Dried chiles
Pasta and rice noodles
Polenta and grits
Popcorn kernels
Posole
Rolled oats
Spices, ground and whole (see list on page 27)
Whole grains, rice, and quinoa

Pared-Down Pots, Pans, and Appliances

Stock the pots and pans that fit the way you cook now, not because you think having a certain set will make you cook in some new and exciting way. All of my pots and pans fit on two long undercounter shelves, and I live under a self-imposed rule that says no new items can come into the house unless something else goes out. If I didn't have that rule, it would be very easy for me to convince myself that I absolutely positively need a 2-quart enameled Dutch oven in a cute color because it would be *so perfect* for making rice! Even though I already have a quality 2-quart pan that is . . . perfect for making rice. When I decided to enter into a long-term relationship with a pressure cooker, for example, I had to liberate a large stainless steel stockpot that was one of the only kitchen tools that my husband brought to our union. One in, one out—that's the rule.

If I had to pare down to the true core of what I need and use the most, I could cook anything I wanted on my personal desert island with these ten items.

Desert Island Equipment

12-inch cast-iron skillet
10-inch stainless steel skillet
8-inch nonstick skillet
8-quart stockpot, with lid
6-quart enameled Dutch oven
6-quart pressure cooker
4-quart saucepan
2-quart saucepan, with lid
2 large rimmed baking sheets
1 cooling rack

You can make nearly all of the recipes in this book with this basic kit. If you are cooking in your first kitchen, this is a great starter pack. If you are a seasoned home cook who has accumulated lots of equipment over the years, try boxing up the things you use infrequently, cooking without them for a few months, and seeing which ones you really miss.

If you cook a lot and want to make room for a few hardworking small appliances, consider these:

10-cup food processor, for making quick work of marinades, blitzing vegetables for sofrito, and making bread crumbs. (There are four recipes in this book that call for a food processor, and two that call for a blender. If you have one machine but not the other, use the one you have.)

High-powered blender, for smoothies and other frozen drinks, obviously, but also for pesto, nut milks, emulsified dressings, and the batter for Birthday-Worthy Swedish Pancakes (page 250).

Toaster oven, for toast (duh), open-face sandwiches, and reheating breaded chicken cutlets and leftover pie. It's also an efficient appliance for toasting small quantities of nuts, roasting vegetables, broiling fresh chiles and garlic for salsas, and revitalizing stale hunks of bread.

How to Live Forever on Fewer Spices

Spices aren't cheap and their flavor is finite—ground spices in particular lose oomph after a month or two, so find ways to use them in your everyday cooking. My spice strategy is about minimizing choices and maximizing usefulness. Edit down to seasonings that are both versatile and pleasing to you, and dip into those jars often, even when a recipe doesn't explicitly tell you to, or any time you're coming up with your own dish. Here's how: Dried spices release their aromatic essences when they're warmed up in fat (oil, butter, drippings, etc.). The first step in most soups, stews, and braises is to slowly sauté chopped vegetables in olive oil, which is a great time to introduce a ground spice such as cumin, fennel, crushed red pepper, cayenne, mustard powder, or turmeric— ½ teaspoon is safe across the board. Add dry spices to marinades. If you're roasting a chicken with salt and pepper, go ahead and include at least one dry spice (I am always reaching for fennel seeds). Warm spices like nutmeg, cinnamon, and cardamom are safe additions to simple baked goods and pancakes. The recipes in this book almost always include suggestions for other spices to use if you don't have the one I've called for; I encourage mixing and matching. Spices, like good olive oil, don't get better with age. Get your money's worth by using them up.

Here are my essential 15 spices along with some ways to cook with them.

The 15 essential spices

Bay leaf

One or two dried bay leaves flutter into every broth, bean, or braise I make. Bay is faintly licorice-y, grassy, and minty, and is one of the few dried herbs worth having. Tuck them into the fat for a confit, or the cavity of a whole chicken for roasting. You could also toss one onto a tray of vegetables before roasting.

Cardamom seeds

Cardamom can be substituted for nutmeg in baked goods or streusel toppings. Infuse ½ teaspoon into dairy-based custards, add to quick breads (banana!) or pound cakes (lemon!); a little bit stirred through a pie filling, especially apple, pear, plum, or blueberry, is magic.

Cayenne

Hot, hot heat! Nothing delivers straight-ahead spiciness quite like cayenne. Anything greater than ½ teaspoon in a recipe for 4 to 6 people will bring a blush to your cheeks. Essential in dry rubs for grilled pork and beef. A dusting will set off rich fatty dishes like deviled eggs and mashed potatoes with zing and flair.

Cinnamon sticks

Try grating about 1 teaspoon cinnamon into vanilla cake batter or chocolate chip cookie dough. A cinnamon stick added to a caramel sauce is a delight, and it also pairs well with lemon and ginger, so put that in a batch of lemonade and call me in the morning. To go savory, simmer this versatile warming spice into vegetable curries and pork and lamb braises.

Coriander seeds

Coriander seeds have citrusy, slightly astringent, cooling properties. They're a classic addition to pickling brines, Moroccan harissa paste, Ethiopian berbere, and garam masala. They're a dream team with cumin and a no-brainer with beans (I'd toast and grind them before adding). Coriander plays well with fish, especially rich fillets of cod, salmon, and sable.

Crushed red pepper

There are a lot of dried chiles in the world, but you'll typically get a medium-spicy cayenne type in a jar of crushed red pepper. I can't imagine spaghetti aglio e olio, lentil soup, meatballs, or marinated feta without it. I also keep Aleppo pepper (its Turkish equivalent), Maras pepper, urfa biber, and gochugaru in the house, each of which has distinct and lovable qualities, and I use them more or less interchangeably.

Cumin (ground)

Cumin and dried beans are made for each other. I also like cumin in my dry spice mixes, especially for steak, pork shoulder and spare ribs, lamb chops, and (sparingly) on shrimp.

Fennel seeds

I love fresh fennel, and I love fennel seeds. If you're not a black licorice person, skip. I combine them 50/50 with crushed red pepper as a seasoning for roast and grilled chicken, and I think fennel is especially delish with turkey and pork. For a soothing tummy tea, steep a big pinch of crushed fennel seeds in boiling water.

Flaky sea salt

Flaky sea salt, unlike kosher salt, is doled out in precise pinches, a last little touch of sparkle, crunch, and—yes, saltiness—on top of salads, sliced roasts and seared steaks, fried eggs, oozy balls of mozzarella, and crudité platters. It's a dessert MVP in sea salt caramels and salty-sweet chocolate chip cookies (or try the Cinnamon Spice and Honey Is Nice Brittle on page 260, or Chocolate and Vanilla Mousse on page 263). If kosher salt is a kitchen's work glove, flaky salt is the cashmere mitten—you might not think you need it, but once you go there, you're never coming back. My favorites are Maldon for its flaky crystallized pyramids; Jacobsen for its moist, crumbly grains; and fleur de sel's crunchy, sturdy nuggets.

Granulated garlic

Yeah, I know: so déclassé. Dried garlic lacks the nuance, aroma, and heat of fresh, and delivers simplified sharp pungency and toasted notes instead. All true. However, I don't think of granulated garlic as a substitute for the real thing—it's its own thing. And a beautiful thing at that! Every time I season a steak, a creamy dip, or roasted potatoes with granulated garlic, I brag about it at work the next day.

Kosher salt and freshly ground pepper

These are the most common seasonings in this book—and in my own cooking—and I even built an entire approach to basic techniques around them (see Salt and Pepper Cooking, page 33). Although the inclusion of salt and pepper in most recipes is treated as a given, in reality, salt is nonnegotiable and pepper is a choice. If you don't care for the bright, sweet, citrusy-piney notes that emanate from freshly ground black pepper, don't use it. (Buying preground pepper is pointless and a waste of money; you're better off using nothing.) Kitchens can't function without kosher salt: It's coarse and grippy enough to be doled out by the pinch and indispensable enough to rain down by the palmful into pasta pots, turkey brines, and pickling liquids. I don't use fine sea salt or iodized salt, and neither one is a 1:1 substitution for kosher.

MSG

Monosodium glutamate is a naturally occurring substance in umami-rich foods: mushrooms, tomatoes, Parmigiano, aged beef, seaweed. Glutamates are legit tasty, and MSG is the synthesized equivalent. If you have a problem with MSG for any reason, take it off this list. If not, shake a few dashes on cucumber salads, noodle soups, fried grains, chicken wings, pork cutlets, sautéed green beans. Just don't @ me for including it.

Mustard seeds

I treasure mustard seeds for their spicy bitterness and their texture. I throw them into sautéed Swiss chard and coat wedges of acorn squash with them before roasting. You can sizzle them in some ghee or olive oil until they start to pop, and spoon the infused mixture, seeds and all, onto any soup or stew for a major value-added finisher. (The yellow ones are less piquant than the brown ones, but I use them interchangeably.)

Pimentón de la Vera

Literally: the true paprika. Spanish pimentón is the OG of the smoked paprika world. Ordinary smoked paprika pretty much exploded into the mainstream a few years ago, and is now easy to find in any grocery store's spice aisle. The import is the couture version. Spanish pimentón ranges from dulce (sweet) to picante (spicy), but even the mildest one has some heat. Add a pinch to eggs, roasted potatoes, paella, and pork (pork meatballs, pork ribs, pork chops, pork stew . . . like, all pork). If you can get the real/*vera* thing, do.

Don't Be So Salty!
My recipes were developed with Diamond Crystal kosher salt. If you use Morton brand, which is almost twice as salty by volume, use half the amount I've called for. Half!

Spin It to Win It

All of the recipes in this book include two shorthand lists at the top of the page that make it easy to see at a glance what ingredients you need. From the Market are the things I think merit an in-person shopping trip. At Home are the items I suggest you order online. As you continue to cook through this book, I hope you'll come to devote your market trips to fun ingredients, and have the functional stuff delivered to your home. Whether you take that advice or not, the recipes will work just the same.

Under the heading Spin It you'll find alternative ingredient options for every single recipe. (Unless otherwise specified, use the same quantity for the replacement ingredient as called for in the recipe.) Spin It is there to remind you that you always have options. Decide for yourself what looks great at the market and buy what makes you hungry. There were days when I was working on these recipes only to discover that I was out of the spice or seasoning I intended to use. Rather than abandoning my mission or making a special trip, I used what I had, because that's exactly what I would want you to do. At home, feel confident about deploying the seasonings you have on hand even if they're not exactly what I called for. Go off script, adapt these recipes to your taste, put your own spin on them, and cook with the ingredients that speak to you. Making adjustments based on what you have on hand or to suit your palate is the mark of a resourceful and confident cook—so if I haven't listed a spin that you think will work, go for it.

Part 2:
The Techniques

Salt and Pepper Cooking

Do More with Less

If there's one thing I've learned from working at *Bon Appétit* all these years, it's that home cooks never complain about short, simple recipes that yield terrific results. Count myself among them. Some of the best things I've ever made—*if I must say so myself*—were seasoned with nothing more than salt and pepper, cooked with extra-virgin olive oil, and zapped with a squeeze of lemon at the end. This is what I call Salt and Pepper Cooking (SPC).

Start with a **main ingredient,** then add four basic seasonings, each of which has a job to do. **Salt and pepper** amplify everything they come into contact with. **Extra-virgin olive oil** carries heat between the pan and the food, mingles with the fats and juices released during cooking, and creates pan sauces and basting liquids. **Fresh lemon juice** balances fat and richness and talks to the part of your palate that detects sour and bitter flavors. All in, that's five ingredients.

"There's nothing in the house to eat" is not going to fly anymore. If you have vegetable oil or butter, you have a replacement for olive oil. Crushed red pepper but no black pepper? You're good. Vinegar or limes instead of lemons? Carry on! The only thing that will stop you is not having salt. If necessary, pinch a child—hard!—and collect his tears. Use those. You're all set.

The Techniques

Six essential, memorizable techniques allow you to cook just about anything. They've all been around for hundreds of years, require no special equipment, and give you total flexibility:

Sauté: moderate to high, dry heat; stovetop; quick

Pan-roast: high, dry heat; stovetop and oven; moderate time

Steam: moderate to high, moist heat; stovetop; quick

Boil and Simmer: high, wet heat; stovetop; moderate time

Confit: low, gentle heat; oven; moderate to slow process

Slow-roast: low, dry or moist heat; oven; extended time

If you accept my assurances that basically all foods can be cooked in a finite, manageable number of ways, you will never again find yourself hesitating over an enticing but unfamiliar ingredient. Crunchy root vegetables are crunchy root vegetables: Anything you do to a carrot you can do to a beet and also to kohlrabi. Quick-cooking proteins are best sautéed or pan-roasted: Treat scallops, fish fillets, thin-cut pork chops, skirt steak, and lamb shoulder chops all the same. With SPC, the seasonings stay the same, the methods are simple, and the main ingredient options are almost endless—treat the six dozen possibilities that appear on the following series of grids as jumping-off points. (Because I believe in dessert, I've included my essential, easy, no-equipment-needed pastry dough as a seventh technique.

When your shopping list is one fun ingredient long and you have confidence in the roster of techniques in your arsenal, you can link the decision about what to buy with a vision of how you want to cook it. There you are, sizing up scallops, winter squash, a pair of artichokes or a dozen ears of corn; tight mushroom clusters, duck breast, a fat steak, a thin steak, new-crop potatoes, purple carrots, chicken thighs. As you settle on what to bring home, mentally scroll through the ways that you could prepare it. Eventually, the roulette wheel stops and the decision is made. That moment, when you feel that spark, when you get the good idea, when you know what you're going to do, is where cooking begins.

No matter what ingredient you're using, refer to the step-by-step photos and captions and follow the visual cues and technical descriptions, even if you're cooking a chicken thigh and the how-to photos show a butternut squash. Times may vary along with the size pan you'll need, but the instructions and process will stay the same. As the ingredient morphs from uncooked to cooked, observe, adjust, smell, listen, and taste everything that's happening. When it pleases you, that's when it's done.

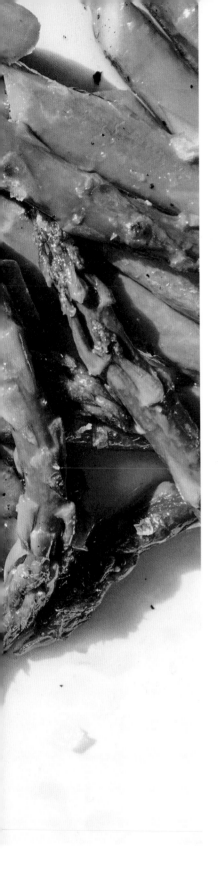

Sauté

Sautéed food is cooked in an oil-slicked skillet over moderately high heat, seasoned with salt and pepper, and subjected to a lot of tossing and stirring, until all of the pieces are lightly browned and just cooked through. This is a stovetop affair, and it shouldn't take long. You can sauté fresh green tender things, like sugar snap peas or zucchini, or crunchy roots, such as radishes, turnips, and carrots. I love sautéed lettuces and leafy greens—from iceberg lettuce to collard greens. Petite proteins like bay scallops, strips of sirloin or pork tenderloin, and nubby pieces of bacon are great things to sauté, too.

Sautéing from Start to Finish

1 If needed, trim ingredient and cut into 1- to 2-inch pieces. The goal is to expose surface areas so that heat from the pan can quickly reach the center of whatever you're cooking.

2 In a skillet that's just big enough to hold your ingredients in a single layer, pour in oil to evenly coat the surface without pooling. Place over medium-high heat until shimmering. Add trimmed ingredient. Listen for immediate sizzle. The pieces should shudder and jump and skitter around a bit. Roll, stir, and toss everything so that all sides make direct contact with the pan.

3 Season with salt and several grinds of black pepper. Unless, of course, you don't like black pepper. (Salt is nonnegotiable, though.) Stir and toss and toss and stir frequently.

4 After a few minutes, you should see golden brown color developing around the edges, and the ingredient will be softening and releasing some moisture. Use a cake tester or your teeth to determine tenderness. Aim for taking the pan off heat when your ingredient has a little bite left to it, but there's no longer any raw tinge. Taste again and adjust the seasoning.

5 Serve with more salt and pepper, a drizzle of olive oil, and a squeeze of lemon.

A Dozen to Sauté

Almonds
Bacon lardons

Asparagus

Fennel
Swiss chard leaves and stems
Mushrooms

Radishes
Scallions
Napa cabbage

Zucchini
Sugar snap peas

Kohlrabi bulbs and stems

Where Cooking Begins

Pan-Roast

Pan-roasting is a high- and dry-heat method that starts on the stovetop and finishes in a hot oven, and is the simplest, most reliable way to achieve beautifully browned surfaces and evenly cooked-through interiors. It is ideal for sturdy, thick-cut foods such as bone-in steaks and chops, slabs of winter squash, whole chickens and bone-in chicken pieces, salmon fillets, large sea scallops, cabbage wedges, cauliflower steaks, and root vegetables. The larger the item, the longer it will take to cook. Scallops might need 2 to 3 minutes, salmon closer to 10, and a flattened chicken will take 30 to 35.

Pan-Roasting from Start to Finish

1 Position a rack in bottom third of oven and preheat to 450°F. In the meantime, prep your ingredient (cut squash into halves or slabs, trim broccoli stems, quarter cabbage, pat chicken dry, etc.).

2 Set a large (10- or 12-inch), dry, heavy skillet over medium heat and let it preheat for 2 to 3 minutes. Meanwhile, generously salt and pepper your ingredient on all sides.

3 When the skillet is hot (a bead of water dropped on the surface should dance and evaporate on contact), increase heat to medium-high and add enough olive oil to coat surface.

4 Add ingredient and press down lightly to ensure good contact with the pan. Cook until the edge where it meets the pan is browned. How long this takes depends on what you're cooking, the pan you're using, and your stove, but start checking after 2 minutes. Reduce the heat if oil is smoking, and add a drizzle of oil if the surface looks dry.

5 Use a thin spatula, pair of tongs, or the tip of a spoon to check the underside of your ingredient. You won't pick up very much additional color in the oven, so make sure you've achieved a dark caramel hue before moving to the next step. Not there yet? Continue cooking in the pan.

6 Turn ingredient onto the second side and press down lightly again, then transfer skillet to the oven. Cook vegetables until tender when pierced with a cake tester, about 10 minutes. (Smaller sea scallops, thin fish fillets, and carrots will cook quickly, 2 to 3 minutes might suffice.)

7 Let meat and poultry rest at least 15 minutes so that juices can redistribute. Serve with fresh lemon for squeezing over, salt, and another drizzle of olive oil.

A Dozen to Pan-Roast

Beets with greens
Carrots
Duck breast

Pork rib chops
Savoy cabbage

Cauliflower

Bone-in beef rib eye
Halved onions

Spatchcock chicken

Salmon steak
Large sea scallops
Butternut squash

Pan-Roast

Steam

Low-fat cooking and other uncool diet trends have given steaming a bad name over the years, but it deserves a full PR makeover. It's a moist cooking technique (obviously) and also a powerful and efficient one because steam is so hot. The combo of high moisture and short cooking time guarantees that whatever you make will never have a chance to dry out. Chicken breasts, mealy if even slightly overcooked, are succulent when steamed. Sweet potatoes take a long time to roast and can get dry and leathery in the process, but they'll be pillow soft and pudding-like after 25 minutes of steaming. If you're afraid of overcooking thin fish fillets, steam them. Steaming is flavor neutral and sets you up to pair whatever you cook with assertive, spicy, sassy, rich, salty, vinegary sauces, condiments, and go-withs. Think spring vegetables with a garlicky aioli. Steamed black bass with vinegar and chili oil. Steamed corn with butter, lime juice, and crushed red pepper. Give steaming some retro love.

Steaming from Start to Finish

1 In a stockpot, bring a few inches of water to a boil, reduce heat to a simmer, and set a steamer basket on top (or fit a steaming rack inside).

2 Lay cleaned and prepped ingredients into basket and season with salt and pepper.

3 Cook until tender when pierced with a cake tester or paring knife. Carrots and like-size vegetables will take about 10 minutes, eggs will take 10 (chill in an ice bath immediately afterwards), and wedges of squash around 14 minutes. Delicate fish fillets and tofu will be done in 5 minutes; figure 15 to 20 minutes for chicken breasts and potatoes.

4 Season with more salt and pepper, olive oil, and a squeeze of lemon.

A Dozen to Steam

Artichoke
Black sea bass

Eggs

Carrots
Corn
Green beans

Kabocha squash
Lobster
Fingerling potatoes

Bok choy
Silken tofu

Boneless chicken breast

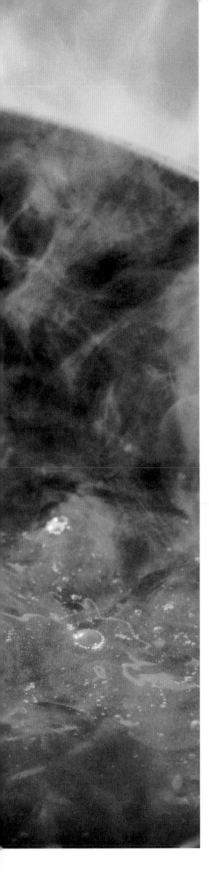

Boil and Simmer

Boiling might be an intermediate step on the way to a finished recipe—cooking wheat berries before adding them to a grain salad, or blanching broccoli rabe to soften it before chopping it and using it in a sauté, for example. But it's also an often-overlooked, forgiving, and totally intuitive process that works for every grain, bean, vegetable, and almost every protein you can think of. Simmering snap beans, flat beans, and peas makes them less starchy and more delicious; shocking them in a bowl of ice water will lock in their color.

The rules are simple: Use a voluminous amount of well-salted water, bring to a boil over high heat, and add your ingredients only when the water reaches a full rolling boil. For everything except eggs, which can boil throughout their cooking time, drop the heat to a simmer. If the water level gets low, add more water. Taste as you go to check for doneness.

Boiling and Simmering from Start to Finish

1 Rice, quinoa, grains, and beans should always be rinsed before cooking. Clean and trim vegetables (scrub potatoes and carrots, stem green beans, peel beets, cut broccoli into spears or florets, etc.).

2 Choose a pot that allows plenty of room for your ingredients to circulate freely, fill it with water, and add a lot of kosher salt (figure ¼ cup kosher salt for every 4 quarts water). This ensures your food will be seasoned all the way through.

3 When you're at a full rolling boil, add your ingredient. Inevitably, the water temperature will drop; bring it back to a boil, then reduce to an active simmer. As long as the pot isn't crowded, getting back to a boil should only take a minute or two.

4   Use a mesh spider or colander to drain ingredients. To keep green vegetables green, transfer to a bowl of ice water to chill. Same for eggs—this will stop the cooking and make them easier to peel. Drain beans, potatoes, or anything else that won't suffer from a touch more cooking time, then spread out on a rimmed baking sheet to cool.

5   Taste and season with olive oil, salt, pepper, and a squeeze of lemon.

A Dozen to Boil and Simmer

Shrimp
Blue potatoes

Wheat berries

Asparagus
Broccoli
Dried cranberry beans

English peas
Green beans
Peaches

Turnips
Eggs

Barley

61   Boil and Simmer

Confit

When you submerge an ingredient in liquefied fat, ideally its own, and cook it slowly and thoroughly in a low oven—that's confit. Once cooked, it can be cooled and then chilled under a blanket of that fat for extended periods of time (it's hermetically sealed under there). Historically and famously, this was done in France with duck *and* goose legs. But the beauty of confit, and the reason I think everyone should be doing it all the time, is that you can use extra-virgin olive oil in place of the rendered animal fat to confit poultry or meat, vegetables (potatoes, fennel, squash), fish (white flaky fishes, tuna and salmon steaks), or whole shallots, small onions, leeks, spring garlic, or ramps (which would be a great way to extend their short spring season).

You can season ingredients that have been confited with more salt and pepper and a squeeze of lemon and eat them up as soon as they come out of the oven. Or you could brown whatever you've made in a skillet over medium heat until the surface is crisp and golden.

At its essence confit is a make-ahead, presentation method. Place the confited ingredient in a clean vessel and pour the strained cooking liquid over it to cover. Cover, then refrigerate; it will hold for weeks. Tease it out of the cold fat on a Tuesday night when you come home starving and remember that you have an incredible thing to eat. Reheat and pair it with a leafy salad, and you will feel like royalty indeed.

Confiting from Start to Finish

1 Clean and trim whatever ingredient you're using. Leeks should be rinsed and dried; carrots, beets, and potatoes scrubbed and dried. Pat dry fish steaks and chicken thighs. Drain canned tomatoes and trim roots of onions and shallots. Preheat oven to 300°F.

2 Season generously with salt and pepper. When using animal proteins, it's ideal to season a day or two ahead to allow flavors to penetrate (keep chilled). If you think of it, great. If not, just push on and it will still be very excellent.

3 Use a cast-iron skillet, Dutch oven, or baking dish that almost isn't big enough to hold the ingredients in a single layer. A little overlap is okay, since whatever you're cooking will shrink as it cooks. A too-big vessel will force you to use more olive oil, and olive oil ain't cheap!

4 Remove a few wide strips of zest from a lemon and twist them over the ingredients to release a spritz of essential oils. Drop the zest into the pan and save the lemon for squeezing the juice over later.

5 Add enough extra-virgin olive oil to *just* cover the ingredient. Don't use an extremely expensive, robustly flavored oil. A fairly mild, buttery and not-too-peppery type in the everyday category is better.

6 Cover pan tightly with foil or a lid and transfer to preheated oven.

7 Cook until the ingredient is absolutely tender all the way through when pierced with a cake tester. Check tuna steaks and large fillets of fish at 45 minutes; leeks, carrots, garlic, or squash pieces after an hour; canned tomatoes, chicken thighs, and turkey legs at 2 hours.

8 Lift ingredients out of cooking liquid and season with a squeeze of lemon and more salt and pepper to serve. Or brown in a skillet over medium heat, turning gently as needed, until golden brown and crisp. Store confited food in a clean container, submerged in strained cooking liquid (add more olive oil if needed to cover).

A Dozen to Confit

Garlic cloves (skin on)
Carrots

Chicken thighs

Fingerling potatoes
Leeks
Lemon

Parsnips
Canned whole tomatoes
Salmon fillets

Turkey legs
Butternut squash

Tuna steak

67   Confit

Slow-Roast

Pan-roasting is hot and fierce. Slow-roasting is low and slow. One major advantage of slow-roasting is simplicity. Anything you can braise—short ribs, pork shoulder, lamb shoulder—you can slow-roast with a fraction of the effort. Unlike braising, you can skip the initial browning (which could take 20 minutes for a hefty cut, like brisket), you don't need a ton of aromatics to infuse the liquid, and you don't need a large volume of stock, or any wine, for that matter. Although slow-roasting essentially is a dry-heat method, it's gentle, and the finished succulent texture is similar to what you'd get with a braise. Meats become shreddable and moist, internal fats and collagen melted into tenderness. Slow-roasting coaxes tough-skinned winter squash into total submission (no peeling, no chopping), yields whole heads of cauliflower soft enough to eat with a spoon, gives whole chickens a rotisserie-esque texture, caramelizes and concentrates juicy things like fennel or sweet peppers, and is the most facile and impressive way to cook large fillets of flaky fish.

Slow-Roasting from Start to Finish

1   Season ingredient aggressively with kosher salt and pepper. A big cut of meat needs a lot of seasoning—1 teaspoon of salt per pound is my standard measure. This can be done 1 to 2 days ahead; refrigerate, uncovered.

2   Preheat oven to 250°F. Place the ingredient in a vessel that holds your ingredient snugly; it will shrink quite a bit while cooking, and too much empty space could lead to overbrowning, dryness, and a tough cleanup job. Add about ¼ cup water to the pot, which will throw off a little steam to start the cooking process.

3   Cover the pot, transfer to the oven, and go take a nap. Set an alarm for 1 hour for smallish vegetables such as shallots, halved onions, or medium-size carrots, and 2 hours for large root vegetables, whole heads of cauliflower or broccoli, and wedges of cabbage. Allow 1 hour for each pound of a large cut of meat (e.g., a 6-pound pork shoulder may take 6 hours).

4 Cook until ingredient is extremely tender but not dried out. If desired, continue cooking, uncovered, to brown surface, 20 to 30 minutes.

5 Serve this delectable-ness with lots of fresh lemon juice squeezed over, more salt and pepper for seasoning, and a drizzle of olive oil, unless there are plenty of pan juices lying about, in which case you should spoon those over.

A Dozen to Slow-Roast

Canned whole tomatoes
St. Louis pork ribs

Hake fillet

Fennel halves
Sweet bell peppers
Cauliflower

Where Cooking Begins

Salmon fillet
Beets with greens
Shallots (unpeeled)

Kabocha squash
Whole chicken

Bone-in pork shoulder roast

Pastry Dough

My essential, beginner-friendly, no-equipment-needed pastry dough is the bonus sweet technique, and you can bake with it year-round. I stumbled upon the unconventional method while watching a vintage episode of *In Julia's Kitchen with Master Chefs*. Julia Child was baking with pastry chef and cookbook author Jim Dodge, whose rolling-pin-enabled pie dough process was so crazy, I had to try it. The results were mind-boggling—the flakiest dough I'd ever made. It looks like a hot mess until you get to the very end, so trust yourself (and me! and Jim! and these photos!) and follow the written cues.

This method does not call for a food processor. You need measuring cups and spoons, and a rolling pin. I use a bench scraper to toss the ingredients together and scrape stuck bits of dough off my countertop and the rolling pin, but a flat metal spatula will get the job done.

I love using this dough to make fruit galettes (see page 242 for my any-fruit recipe). I love galettes because the more messed-up the dough looks when you roll it out, the cooler the pastry comes out in the end. If you want a more polished look or want to make a tart, transfer the dough to a pie dish or a 10-inch removable-bottom tart pan. You can also use this dough for a double-crust pie; just double the recipe and divide it into two disks. Allow 90 minutes baking time, and shield the top crust with a ring of foil after 45 minutes if it is browning too quickly.

Pastry Dough from Start to Finish

1   Dump 1¾ cups all-purpose flour onto a clean work surface, add 1 teaspoon kosher salt and 1 teaspoon sugar, and toss with your fingers to distribute.

2   Toss 8 ounces cold unsalted butter, cut into 10 or 12 pieces, into the dry ingredients to coat each piece.

3   Use a rolling pin to roll the butter into the flour until it is in long, thin pieces. This will take several passes to achieve. Use a bench scraper to help corral the mixture as you go, and to scrape the work surface and rolling pin clean if butter and flour stick to it.

4   Work quickly so that the butter stays cold but becomes malleable. When the butter pieces are flattened into thin pieces, you've arrived. If you go too far, the butter will soften and start to melt, and you'll struggle with the next step.

5 Drizzle ¼ cup ice water over and use a bench scraper and your hands to toss mixture together until water is distributed, then roll out dough to a long rectangle with short ends about 10 inches wide.

6 Using the bench scraper, fold the top third of the dough over the middle, then lift up the bottom third and fold that up and over (as though you were folding a letter into thirds). Rotate the dough 90 degrees and repeat rolling and folding, gathering loose bits in with the main part of the dough as you go.

7 After rotating the dough 90 degrees and rolling and folding a third time, the dough should be a little crumbly along the sides, but smooth in the center, and will hold together when you squeeze a piece in your palm. If not, repeat rolling and folding again. Gather dough into a disk, then wrap in plastic wrap and press down to 1 inch thick. Chill dough for at least 30 minutes and up to 2 days before rolling out. (Dough can be frozen for up to 3 months.)

One Dough for Eight Galettes

Apple

Banana

Plum

Blood orange

Fig
Rhubarb–strawberry

Blueberry–blackberry
Pear

Pastry Dough

Part 3:
The Recipes

Cook with Abandon

Starring Produce

These recipes start with a trip to the market and take shape when you get home with a bag full of things that came out of the ground. They're plant-based but dinner-worthy, and can be made in an hour or less.

Spring lettuces with anchovy cream	84
Mozzarella with charred and raw sugar snap peas	87
Savory summer melon salad	88
Pan-roasted Romanesco with toasted nuts and crispy bits	91
Buttery beets and grapefruit	92
Chicories with garlic bread croutons	95
Fresh figs with Manchego and wet walnuts	96
Salted cucumbers with ginger and chile	99
Coconutty collards slaw	100
Ham-and-butter baguette with green beans	103
Stir-fried celery with peanuts and bacon	104
Charred broccoli salad	107
Leeks with potato chips and chives	108
Grilled asparagus with smoky-spicy brown-butter bread crumbs	111
Sweet potatoes with tahini butter	112

Spring lettuces with anchovy cream

This dressing was inspired by the Italian sauce called bagna cauda, a warm olive oil dip in which anchovies, capers, garlic, parsley, and nuts take a nice bath. I wanted something luscious and rich to temper those sharp and salty ingredients, and really struggled before landing on the creamiest thing of all: cream. Steeping the garlic and anchovy with the cream mellows their bite, while simultaneously infusing the cream with flavor. Everybody wins!

4 to 6 servings

From the Market
Heavy cream
Parsley
Lettuce

Spin It
2 heads Little Gem romaine hearts, 2 heads Boston lettuce, or 1 head green or red leaf lettuce can all be used
1 head radicchio or 3 endive for the lettuce

At Home
Anchovy fillets
Garlic
Salt and pepper
Walnuts
Olive oil
Red wine vinegar
Flaky sea salt

Spin It
A few dashes of fish sauce for anchovies
Almonds or pecans in place of walnuts
Lemon juice for vinegar

⅔ cup heavy cream
2 oil-packed anchovy fillets
½ bunch parsley, stems and leaves separated, leaves roughly chopped
3 garlic cloves, smashed
Kosher salt, freshly ground pepper
⅔ cup walnuts, roughly chopped
¼ cup extra-virgin olive oil
2 small heads lettuce, leaves separated, washed, and dried
2 teaspoons red wine vinegar
Flaky sea salt, for serving

In a small saucepan, combine cream, anchovies, parsley stems, garlic, a pinch of salt, and several grinds of pepper and bring to a very gentle simmer over medium heat. Remove from heat, cover, and let sit 10 minutes for flavors to infuse.

Meanwhile, in a small skillet, combine walnuts and olive oil and cook over medium heat, tossing and stirring often, until nuts are deep golden and toasty in spots, about 3 minutes. Transfer to a small bowl, season with salt, and stir. Let cool.

Pluck the parsley stems out of the cream mixture, then use a fork to whisk the mixture and break the garlic and anchovies into small pieces (the fillets should disintegrate without any effort). Taste dressing and season with salt, if needed.

Toss lettuce in a large serving bowl or platter with vinegar, then season with flaky salt. Spoon dressing over (use all of it even though it might seem like a lot). Stir walnuts and chopped parsley together and scatter over the salad. Season with more flaky salt and pepper.

Mozzarella with charred and raw sugar snap peas

Just-picked sugar snap peas are sweet, firm, and juicy, and have no starchiness to them. They're completely enjoyable raw, but charring gives the edible pods a little unexpected smoky bitterness. This dish lets you have it both ways, along with plenty of creamy cheese to play up the crunchiness of the peas.

6 servings

From the Market
Mozzarella
Sugar snap peas
Crusty bread

Spin It
Green beans, cherry tomatoes, or radishes in place of snap peas
Fresh ricotta instead of mozzarella
Crushed red pepper stirred into olive oil instead of Calabrian chiles

At Home
Olive oil
Flaky sea salt
Salt and pepper
Lemon
Crushed Calabrian chiles in oil

Spin It
Toasted sesame oil or hazelnut oil instead of Calabrian chiles or olive oil

2 (8-ounce) balls buffalo mozzarella or 1 (1-pound) ball salted fresh mozzarella
Extra-virgin olive oil, for drizzling and brushing
Flaky sea salt
1 pound sugar snap peas, trimmed
Kosher salt, freshly ground pepper
6 thick-cut slices crusty bread, such as miche
1 lemon
Crushed Calabrian chiles in oil, for serving

Hot to Trot
Jarred Calabrian chiles, from the southernmost region of Italy, are molto spicy and intensely flavored. If you love hot stuff, they're worth a try. You can find them at specialty grocers and online.

Place mozzarella on a serving platter, drizzle with olive oil, and season with flaky salt. Let sit at room temperature at least 1 hour before serving to take off the chill, which is key for creamy oozy insides and the best flavor. (In a perfect world, that mozzarella would never have been refrigerated, but these are imperfect times.)

Prepare a grill for medium-high direct heat.

In a medium bowl, drizzle sugar snap peas with some olive oil and toss to coat. Season with salt and pepper. Set a wire rack or grill basket on grill, add half of peas, and grill, tossing occasionally, until charred in spots, about 3 minutes. (Or, char half the peas in a dry cast-iron skillet over high heat.) Return peas to bowl with raw ones and toss to combine.

Generously brush both sides of bread with olive oil. Grill until lightly toasted, about 2 minutes (or use a dry cast-iron skillet over medium-high heat). Holding the uncut lemon in one hand, rub the lemon peel vigorously against the surface of the toast to pick up some of the zest and release some essential oils. Cut the bread into quarters or rectangular soldiers.

Add peas to platter with cheese and drizzle more olive oil over everything. Spoon up some of the chiles and their oil and drizzle over. Serve with spoons for the cheese, along with grilled bread and flaky salt for making perfect bites.

Savory summer melon salad

When some melons are at their peak, they can be insanely aromatic and very sweet. I've always loved savory preparations for that reason—think cantaloupe with prosciutto or lots of black pepper, watermelon with feta, honeydew with salt and olive oil. All delicious. This is in the same vein—the fish sauce adds saltiness and umami, the melon is sweet but also vegetal (it's a gourd, like squash and cucumber), and the lime has the zing. You can skip the MSG if you want, but I wouldn't.

4 servings

From the Market
Melon
Basil

Spin It
Any ripe melon, such as Galia, Charentais, Crenshaw, or Sharlyn melon
An equivalent weight of seedless or Sugar Baby watermelon will work for the melon
Mint and/or cilantro instead of basil

At Home
Lime
Fish sauce
Flaky sea salt
Cayenne
MSG
Olive oil

Spin It
Soy sauce in place of sea salt
Small fresh red or green chiles in place of cayenne
Toasted sesame oil in place of olive oil

1 (1½-pound) orange-, yellow-, or green-fleshed summer melon, such as cantaloupe or honeydew, chilled, rind washed
3 tablespoons fresh lime juice
2 teaspoons fish sauce
Handful of Thai or Italian basil leaves
Flaky sea salt, cayenne, MSG, and extra-virgin olive oil, for serving

Halve the melon and scoop out seeds, taking care not to remove all of the tender flesh immediately surrounding the seeds themselves, which is usually the most concentrated and delicious part of the fruit. Using a soup spoon, scoop out melon flesh in large irregular pieces onto a rimmed platter or bowl until you get down to the rind.

Season the melon with lime juice and fish sauce and toss very gently to combine. Add half the basil and fold through, then season with flaky salt, a pinch of cayenne, and a few dashes of MSG. Drizzle with olive oil and top with remaining basil. Let sit for a few minutes for juices to release before serving.

Pan-roasted Romanesco with toasted nuts and crispy bits

Romanesco shows up in the late fall, tastes like a cross between cauliflower and broccoli, and is studded with fractal-shaped florets that make it look like a magical mythical structure. In this recipe I cut it into steaks and roast it in slabs until tender, and the loose pieces of florets get super browned and crunchy. It's a texture party.

4 servings

From the Market
Romanesco
Parsley

Spin It
Cauliflower or broccoli
   for Romanesco
Cilantro or mint instead
   of parsley

At Home
Salt
Olive oil
Butter
Hazelnuts
Garlic
White wine vinegar
Flaky sea salt
Lemon

Spin It
Almonds or cashews for
   hazelnuts
Unseasoned rice vinegar
   or cider vinegar for
   the wine vinegar
Lime instead of lemon

---

1 medium head Romanesco
   (1½ pounds), stem trimmed
Kosher salt
2 tablespoons extra-virgin olive
   oil, plus more for drizzling
2 tablespoons unsalted butter
¼ cup skin-on or blanched
   hazelnuts, roughly chopped
2 garlic cloves, sliced
2 teaspoons white wine vinegar
½ cup chopped fresh parsley
   leaves and tender stems
Flaky sea salt
Lemon wedges, for serving

Preheat oven to 400°F.

Stand Romanesco on its stem and cut it from top to bottom into 1- to 1½-inch-thick slabs. You should get 3 or 4 intact pieces. Don't worry about the rounded outer edges that may crumble or any small florets that break away in large pieces, just scoot those to one side of the cutting board along with any nice-looking leaves; you'll use everything. Cut the loose bits into ½-inch pieces and season them and the Romanesco steaks with salt.

Heat a 10- or 12-inch cast-iron skillet over medium-high heat. Drizzle 2 tablespoons oil into the skillet and slip Romanesco steaks into pan—you might have to puzzle them together, but make sure they don't overlap. Work in batches if needed. Cook until Romanesco is dark brown on the underside, about 6 minutes. Turn over and drizzle a bit more oil over the second side and into the empty areas of the pan. Scatter the chopped pieces of Romanesco into the spaces between the steaks and toss gently to lightly coat them with oil (add more if needed).

Transfer pan to oven and roast until a cake tester inserted into stem slips through without much effort, 15 to 18 minutes. Steaks should be firm enough to still hold together without being crunchy.

Use a spatula to transfer steaks to a large plate or platter. Return pan with loose pieces of Romanesco to medium-high heat. Add butter, hazelnuts, and garlic and cook, stirring, until everything is toasted and crisp around edges, about 4 minutes. Add vinegar and parsley and quickly stir up any browned bits. Spoon this mixture over the steaks, season with flaky salt, and serve with lemon wedges for squeezing over.

Buttery beets and grapefruit

This is a riff on scallops with brown butter and lemon, but with beets instead of scallops and grapefruit in place of lemon. I prefer good old-fashioned white or oro blanco grapefruit for its high acidity; if you're using a ruby red, which is sweeter, shake a few extra drops of cider vinegar over the dish right before serving.

6 servings

From the Market
Grapefruit
Shallot
Beets
Mint

Spin It
Any color beets will work
Cilantro instead of mint

At Home
Ginger
Salt
Flaky sea salt
Cider vinegar
Toasted sesame oil
Olive oil
Butter

Spin It
Unseasoned rice vinegar or sherry vinegar instead of cider vinegar

1 white grapefruit
4-inch piece fresh ginger, peeled and finely grated
1 shallot, very thinly sliced
Kosher salt
1 teaspoon cider vinegar
1 teaspoon toasted sesame oil, plus more for drizzling
3 softball-size beets (about 1½ pounds), trimmed, scrubbed, peeled, and cut into 1- to 1½-inch-thick wedges
2 tablespoons extra-virgin olive oil
Flaky sea salt
3 tablespoons unsalted butter
Mint leaves, for serving

Prep the grapefruit, which you're going to use three ways: First, use a vegetable peeler to remove 3 or 4 long wide strips of zest, avoiding the bitter white pith underneath. Set zest aside. Next, take off a thin slice from the top and bottom of grapefruit and upend it on a cut side. Using a thin sharp knife and following the curve of the fruit, cut away peel and pith to expose flesh. Slice off a 2-inch-thick round from one end of grapefruit and squeeze juice from that piece into a small bowl; you'll have about 2 tablespoons. Slice remaining grapefruit crosswise into ½-inch-thick rounds and transfer to a platter. Pick out seeds.

Put ginger into a small mesh sieve set over bowl with grapefruit juice and press down on solids so that ginger juice drips into bowl. Set grapefruit-ginger juice aside (discard solids).

Place shallot slices in a small bowl, cover with cold water, and use your fingertips to separate into individual rings. Soak for 5 minutes, then drain and return to same bowl. Season with salt and add vinegar and 1 teaspoon sesame oil. Set pickled shallots aside.

Season beets with salt. In a large skillet, heat olive oil over medium-high heat until shimmering. Place beets in pan with a flat side down. Cook until almost charred underneath, 6 to 8 minutes, shaking skillet occasionally to make sure they aren't sticking. Turn beets and cook on second flat side until golden brown, 4 to 5 minutes. Cut into one and taste to check doneness—it should be firm at the center, but no longer completely raw. Transfer to platter with grapefruit and tuck grapefruit slices between and around beet wedges. Season with flaky salt. Let skillet cool for 2 to 3 minutes.

Pour off any oil from skillet and carefully wipe out with paper towel. Return to medium heat, add grapefruit-ginger juice, swirl, and cook just until mixture simmers (this will happen almost immediately). Add butter and reserved zest and cook until butter is browned and smells nutty, about 4 minutes (if you're using a pan with a dark surface, spoon a little onto a white plate to check color).

Spoon pan sauce over beets and grapefruit. Top with pickled shallots, along with any juices in bowl. Serve topped with mint.

Chicories with garlic bread croutons

When we first met, my husband claimed to not like bitter greens, and was skeptical of radicchio, escarole, arugula—even endive. Because those are some of my most beloved leafy things, I felt it was my duty to show him The Way. This particular way is to create a booby trap of cheesy, garlicky croutons that tuck themselves inside the ruffled and resilient lettuces, creating unavoidable, forkable opportunities.

4 servings

From the Market
Chicory lettuces
Crusty bread
Oregano

Spin It
Any other chicories,
    such as escarole,
    mature arugula, and/
    or Castelfranco

At Home
Olive oil
Garlic
Parmigiano
Crushed red pepper
Salt and pepper
Red wine vinegar
Sugar

Spin It
Grana Padano,
    Pecorino Romano, or
    nutritional yeast for
    the Parmigiano
Sherry vinegar or cider
    vinegar for the red
    wine vinegar

3 small heads chicory lettuce,
    such as radicchio, Treviso,
    and/or endive
⅓ cup extra-virgin olive oil, plus
    more for drizzling
4 thick slices crusty bread, such
    as miche
1 small garlic clove, peeled
½ cup coarsely grated Parmigiano
1 teaspoon fresh oregano, roughly
    chopped
Crushed red pepper
Kosher salt, freshly ground pepper
¼ cup red wine vinegar
1 teaspoon sugar

Separate lettuces into individual leaves, wash, and dry. Chill until ready to serve.

Drizzle some olive oil over both sides of bread and toast until dark golden brown, about 5 minutes. Rub with garlic clove, then tear into large pieces. While still warm, toss croutons in a medium bowl with Parmigiano, oregano, and crushed red pepper to coat. Season croutons with salt and black pepper.

In a serving bowl, whisk together vinegar and sugar until sugar dissolves. Season with salt and pepper, then stream in ⅓ cup olive oil. The dressing will be extra vinegary, which will balance the bitterness of the greens. Add greens to bowl, season with salt and pepper, and toss gently but thoroughly with your hands to coat. Add croutons, then toss again to combine.

Fresh figs with Manchego and wet walnuts

Is it an appetizer? A savory fruit salad? Could it pass as dessert? Does it belong on a cheese board? Will you want to eat just the walnut part with a spoon, alone, and in private? Yes.

4 servings

From the Market
Manchego
Figs

Spin It
Parmigiano, aged Gouda, or aged cheddar instead of Manchego
Ripe pears or persimmons instead of figs

At Home
Walnuts
Olive oil
Honey
Salt and pepper
Unseasoned rice vinegar

Spin It
Almonds or pistachios instead of walnuts
Maple syrup instead of honey
Lemon juice for the vinegar

½ cup roughly chopped walnut halves
3 tablespoons extra-virgin olive oil
1 tablespoon honey
Kosher salt, freshly ground pepper
2 teaspoons unseasoned rice vinegar, divided
6 ounces Manchego
2 pints dead-ripe fresh figs

In a small skillet, toast walnuts in olive oil over medium heat, stirring frequently, until golden brown and toasted, about 5 minutes. Remove from heat and stir in honey to combine. Season with salt and lots (and lots) of pepper. Add 1 teaspoon rice vinegar and taste again. The dressing should be sweet and fatty and lip-smacky and peppery. Adjust as needed with more honey, oil, salt, pepper, and/or vinegar, until you're pleased.

Break up the Manchego into pieces that roughly mimic the size and shape of the walnuts. Tear figs in half and place on a large plate or platter. Season with salt and remaining 1 teaspoon vinegar. Tuck in pieces of cheese here and there, then spoon walnut dressing over. The best thing that could happen is that you'd get the perfect piece of fig with a wet walnut tucked into it and a piece of cheese attached, and you'd eat it with your hands. Keep eating until that happens.

Salted cucumbers with ginger and chile

Cucumbers are literally thirst-quenching, and you can find salads that celebrate them in cuisines as far-reaching as Chinese, Korean, Japanese, Greek, Taiwanese, Israeli, Iranian, and Turkish, to name a few. Salt unlocks the cucumbers' moisture and seasons them, and their fresh, sweet, grassy flavor is perfectly suited to the bright and acidic ingredients.

4 to 6 servings

From the Market
English cucumbers
Fresno chile

Spin It
8 Persian (mini) cucumbers in place of English, halved crosswise and then quartered lengthwise
Jalapeño or half a Thai chile in place of Fresno (or omit)

At Home
Salt
Ginger
Garlic
Unseasoned rice vinegar

Spin It
Cider vinegar or lime juice instead of rice vinegar

2 English hothouse cucumbers
Kosher salt
2-inch piece fresh ginger, peeled, finely grated
1 small garlic clove, finely grated
1 tablespoon unseasoned rice vinegar
1 small Fresno chile, finely grated

Trim ends of cucumber and use a vegetable peeler to remove the skin in alternating strips so that you create a striped effect. Cut cucumbers crosswise into thirds, then cut each third lengthwise into quarters or sixths. Put cucumbers in a colander set in the sink or over a bowl and toss with a generous sprinkling of salt. Let sit for 20 to 30 minutes to season the cucumbers and draw out some of their moisture. Pat dry.

Put the cucumbers in a serving bowl and add ginger and garlic. Add vinegar and about half the chile and toss to combine. Taste and adjust seasoning with more chile and salt, as desired.

Coconutty collards slaw

If you took part in the kale salad phenomenon circa 2010, you've probably massaged your fair share of those hardy greens. Firmly squeezing kale leaves crushes their cell walls, which tenderizes them and makes them a pleasure to eat when raw. The same thing happens with collards (they're related). They become softened but are still sturdy enough to make ahead and pack for a potluck, a picnic, the beach, or a plane; just don't add the coconut flakes until you're ready to eat.

6 servings

From the Market
Collard greens
Serrano chile

Spin It
Green cabbage, Tuscan kale, or red Russian kale for the collards
Fresno or jalapeño chile for the serrano

At Home
Salt
Lime
Coconut flakes
Crushed red pepper
Coconut milk
Garlic
Unseasoned rice vinegar
Sugar
Fish sauce

Spin It
Chopped peanuts in place of coconut flakes
Cider vinegar or white distilled vinegar for rice vinegar
Kimchi juice (from jar of kimchi) instead of fish sauce

1 small bunch collard greens, preferably with small leaves (12 ounces)
Kosher salt
3 tablespoons fresh lime juice
1 cup unsweetened coconut flakes
½ teaspoon crushed red pepper
½ cup unsweetened coconut milk, shaken
1 small serrano chile, thinly sliced (seeds removed if you want less heat)
1 small garlic clove, finely grated
3 tablespoons unseasoned rice vinegar
1 teaspoon sugar
Fish sauce, for seasoning

Cut out the collard stems and center ribs, then cut leaves into 1- to 2-inch-wide strips. Stack strips and cut crosswise into ½-inch lengths. Transfer to a serving bowl or platter, season with salt, add lime juice, and massage collards, tossing and squeezing them like you mean it, until they are bright green and juicy, about 3 minutes. Set collard mixture aside.

Heat a small skillet over medium. Add coconut flakes and cook, tossing often, until they are golden brown, 1 to 2 minutes. Add crushed red pepper and season with salt, then immediately transfer to a plate to cool (they may darken a shade or two and will crisp as they cool).

In a small bowl, whisk together coconut milk, serrano, garlic, vinegar, and sugar. Season to taste with a few dashes of fish sauce (which is both salty and funky) and more salt, if needed.

Pour coconut dressing over collards and toss to combine. Serve topped with toasted coconut.

Ham-and-butter baguette with green beans

One summer a couple of years ago I started bringing bread and butter to the beach along with any cooked vegetables that were left over from dinner the night before. And that, my friends, is how I ended up sticking green beans into a sandwich for the first time. It would not be the last.

2 generous servings

From the Market
Green beans
Baguette
Ham
Comté or Gruyère

Spin It
Thinly sliced cucumbers
or radishes (do not
pour water over) for
green beans
Prosciutto or thinly
sliced salami for ham

At Home
Flaky sea salt
Butter
Dijon mustard
Horseradish

4 ounces thin green beans,
stems trimmed
Flaky sea salt
1 baguette or 2 demi-baguettes
4 tablespoons (2 ounces) unsalted
butter, at room temperature
2 tablespoons Dijon mustard
2 tablespoons prepared
horseradish
4 ounces thinly sliced ham
2 ounces Comté or Gruyère,
shaved with a vegetable peeler

Bring a kettle of water to a boil. Put green beans in a shallow bowl or pie plate and pour hot water over them to cover. Let sit 5 minutes to soften, then drain and pat dry. Season with salt.

Split baguette lengthwise. Spread butter on both cut sides and season with salt. Spread mustard on one side and horseradish on the other. Drape ham onto bottom half, top with beans, then cheese. Firmly press sandwich closed before cutting crosswise.

Stir-fried celery with peanuts and bacon

Celery—so divisive! I honestly don't know what it is about the noisily crunchy stalks, but some of my favorite people absolutely hate the stuff. Because I'm stubborn, I keep trying to come up with recipes that will turn the haters into lovers. Deploying bacon and peanuts seemed like a good place to start.

4 servings

From the Market
Celery
Green cabbage

Spin It
Fennel or Brussels
 sprouts for the celery
Omit the celery and
 double the cabbage
Kohlrabi or cauliflower
 (thinly sliced) for the
 cabbage

At Home
Bacon
Peanuts
Salt
Soy sauce
Unseasoned rice
 vinegar
Chili oil

Spin It
Pancetta or pork
 sausage meat for
 the bacon
Hot sauce for the
 chili oil

½ **bunch celery or 2 celery**
 hearts (½ pound)
2 **ounces thick-cut bacon, cut**
 crosswise into ½-inch pieces
½ **cup salted roasted peanuts**
¼ **head green cabbage, leaves**
 torn into 1-inch pieces
Kosher salt
1 **teaspoon soy sauce**
1 **teaspoon unseasoned rice**
 vinegar
Chili oil, for serving

Cut celery stalks crosswise on a long diagonal into ¼-inch pieces. Snap off the light green celery leaves from the innermost stalks and set those aside.

Place bacon in a large cold skillet, then place over medium heat. Cook, stirring occasionally, until bacon renders most of its fat and starts to curl up and turn golden but is nowhere near crisp, about 5 minutes. Add peanuts, increase heat to medium-high, and cook, stirring frequently, until peanuts take on some color, about 2 minutes. Add celery and cabbage, season lightly with salt, and cook, tossing, just until celery is browned in spots but still crunchy, and the cabbage is bright green and tender, but still has some bite to it, about 4 minutes. Add soy sauce and vinegar and toss through.

Transfer to a serving platter. Drizzle with chili oil and top with reserved celery leaves.

Charred broccoli salad

Searing broccoli lets you straddle the line between raw and cooked in this crunchy salad. I like rich, buttery Marcona almonds against the rustic broccoli, but regular almonds will work, too. Because the broccoli is so sturdy, this dish holds well, and the dates will continue to soften and absorb flavor as time goes on. It's a good one to make ahead for dinner, or take to a friend's place.

4 servings

From the Market
Broccoli
Medjool dates
Cheddar
Marcona almonds

Spin It
Cauliflower for broccoli
Golden raisins or dried
    sour cherries for the
    dates
Parmigiano or
    Manchego for the
    cheddar
Any other toasted
    salted nut in place of
    almonds

At Home
Olive oil
Salt and pepper
Cider vinegar
Honey

Spin It
Unseasoned rice
    vinegar or
    sherry vinegar for
    cider vinegar

2 broccoli heads (about
    1½ pounds)
5 teaspoons extra-virgin olive oil,
    divided
Kosher salt, freshly ground pepper
1 tablespoon cider vinegar, plus
    more to taste
6 Medjool dates, pitted and
    roughly chopped
2 ounces aged or sharp cheddar,
    shaved with a vegetable peeler
½ cup salted Marcona almonds,
    roughly chopped
1 teaspoon honey, plus more
    to taste

Trim woody ends from broccoli stalks, then cut heads away from stems. Peel stems and halve lengthwise. Cut broccoli heads in half through the crown to create two lobes (don't separate into individual florets).

Heat a large cast-iron skillet over medium-high heat. Add 2 teaspoons oil to pan. Season broccoli pieces all over with salt and pepper, then place in skillet, cut sides down. Cook, undisturbed, until undersides are well browned but broccoli is still crunchy (a cake tester should meet firm resistance when inserted into thick part of stem), 4 to 5 minutes. Turn heads onto floret side for a minute, just to lightly brown rounded sides, then transfer to a cutting board.

When cool enough to handle, cut broccoli heads and stems into ¼-inch slices and transfer to a medium serving bowl. Add vinegar, dates, cheddar, and almonds. Season with salt and pepper and toss gently to coat. Add honey and remaining 3 teaspoons oil and toss again. Spear yourself a forkful with all components accounted for; it should be a balanced, well seasoned mix of crunchy, chewy, sweet, bitter, and sour. If not, tweak seasoning until it pleases you.

Leeks with potato chips and chives

Everyone should be topping more things with potato chips. They're salty. They're crunchy. They're naturally gluten-free! It's a zero-effort crouton situation. I like the kettle style because they have some structure to them. Tuck them into sandwiches and burgers, or crumble them onto hot dogs, fried rice, or split pea soup.

4 servings

From the Market
Leeks
Potato chips
Chives

Spin It
Red onions, quartered,
   for the leeks
Corn chips or corn nuts
   in place of potato
   chips
Parsley, cilantro, and/or
   mint instead of chives

At Home
Salt and pepper
Ghee

Spin It
Coconut oil or a 50/50
   mix of vegetable oil
   and butter for the
   ghee

4 leeks, trimmed and halved
   lengthwise
Kosher salt, freshly ground pepper
3 tablespoons ghee
1 cup kettle-cooked potato chips
¼ cup finely sliced chives

Rinse leeks, pat them dry, and season all over with salt and pepper. Heat a large, dry skillet, preferably cast-iron, over medium-high heat for 2 minutes. Add leeks to pan, cut side down, and cook, shaking pan occasionally, until evenly charred on cut side, about 4 minutes (charred is a nice way of saying burned; things could get a little smoky).

Turn leeks over and add ghee and ⅔ cup water to the skillet. Reduce to a simmer and cook until leeks are tender when pierced with a cake tester and liquid is almost completely evaporated, about 4 minutes longer. Transfer leeks to a serving plate. Crush potato chips with your hands and let the pieces rain down on the leeks, then top with chives.

Grilled asparagus with smoky-spicy brown-butter bread crumbs

Piment d'esplette, a prized crushed chile from France's Basque region, is a little bit like saffron: It's expensive, but for good reason. The peppers are harvested by hand and air-dried, and it's possible you can detect a whiff of French sunshine mixed in with their restrained delicate heat. (I made that last part up.) Grilled asparagus is one of the things I look forward to most when spring produce finally shows up on the East Coast, and I choose to honor the occasion by tossing fancy spiced bread crumbs all over the place.

4 servings

From the Market
Piment d'Espelette
Crusty bread
Asparagus

Spin It
1 teaspoon Aleppo pepper or chili powder instead of piment d'Espelette
Savoy or napa cabbage leaves, halved, Romano beans, wax beans or string beans, for the asparagus

At Home
Butter
Paprika
Salt and pepper
Olive oil

Spin It
Ghee or olive oil for butter
Ground cumin or crushed fennel for paprika

8 tablespoons (4 ounces) unsalted butter
2 teaspoons piment d'Espelette
½ teaspoon sweet paprika
Kosher salt
2 cups torn bread from the center of a sturdy loaf
1 pound medium-to-large asparagus, tough ends snapped off
Extra-virgin olive oil, for coating
Freshly ground pepper

Prepare a grill for medium-high indirect heat (for a charcoal grill, bank coals to one side; for a gas grill, leave one set of burners off). Clean and lightly oil grates.

In a 10-inch cast-iron skillet, combine butter, piment d'Espelette, paprika, and a big pinch of salt. Place skillet on cooler side of grill and cook, stirring occasionally to incorporate spices, until the butter is foaming, about 3 minutes. Add the torn bread and stir well to coat. Continue to cook, sliding pan onto hotter part of grill as needed to keep things sizzling along, until

croutons are very toasty and crisp and butter smells nutty (don't let it burn), about 6 minutes. Set aside. (You can also do this on a stove.)

Toss asparagus with olive oil to coat, then season with salt and pepper. Grill over direct heat until asparagus is charred in spots, bright green, hot to the center, and crunchy-juicy, about 4 minutes. Do not overcook. (Alternatively, broil asparagus on a rimmed baking sheet, 3 to 4 minutes.)

Serve asparagus topped with bread crumbs.

Sweet potatoes with tahini butter

The first time I made this dish I wrote a note to myself that said "Yum! Not much to look at, but yum." You will have extra tahini butter left over: Scrape it into a jar and chill it. It will keep for at least a week and is an easy dinner fixer. Toss it with warm grains, udon noodles, or a tray of roasted vegetables; spread it onto a seared steak while it rests, or use it to top broiled salmon or snapper.

6 servings

From the Market
Sweet potatoes

Spin It
Acorn or butternut
　squash, cut into
　2-inch wedges,
　in place of sweet
　potatoes

At Home
Butter
Tahini
Soy sauce
Toasted sesame oil
Lime
Salt and pepper
Flaky sea salt
Sesame seeds

Spin It
Creamy peanut butter
　for tahini
Walnut oil in place of
　sesame oil
Unseasoned rice
　vinegar for lime juice
Crushed toasted
　peanuts or pepitas for
　sesame seeds

3 pounds sweet potatoes, any
　color (6 small or 3 large),
　scrubbed
6 tablespoons unsalted butter,
　at room temperature
2 tablespoons tahini
1 tablespoon soy sauce
2 teaspoons toasted
　sesame oil
¼ cup fresh lime juice, plus
　wedges for serving
Kosher salt, freshly ground pepper
Flaky sea salt and toasted sesame
　seeds, for serving

Bring a few inches of water to a boil in a medium stockpot fitted with a steamer basket. Halve the sweet potatoes crosswise if large and place them in the steamer. Cover, reduce the heat to medium, and steam until potatoes are completely tender, about 30 minutes. I use a cake tester to check doneness, but the tines of a fork or tip of a paring knife would work, too.

Meanwhile, in a small bowl, combine the butter, tahini, soy sauce, sesame oil, and lime juice and use a spatula, spoon, or fork to smash them together (you will think the butter and the liquids will never fully combine, but don't give up—it will happen). Season tahini butter with salt and a generous amount of pepper.

Use tongs to transfer cooked potatoes to a large plate or platter. When just cool enough to handle, split potatoes in half and spread tahini butter generously onto flesh. Don't be skimpy: The tahini butter is a sauce, not a schmear. Top with a liberal coating of sesame seeds and season with flaky salt. Serve with more lime wedges—these really come alive with lots of bright citrus.

Egg-centric

These decidedly savory recipes prove that
the addition of an egg is all that's needed
to push a side dish onto center stage.

Slow-cooked dozen-egg frittata	117
BLTs with bacon-fat fried eggs	118
Omelet with whipped ricotta for two	121
Poached egg and silky braised greens	122
Fried grains with bacon, mushrooms, and kimchi	125
Aioli and all the things for dipping	126
Carbonara stracciatella	131

Slow-cooked dozen-egg frittata

Until I came across the slow-cook frittata method from the legendary Brooklyn pizzeria Franny's, I'd always cooked them over medium-high heat on the stovetop and then flashed them under the broiler to brown the top side at the end. This gentle-heat process creates a dense and creamy texture, and it made me an instant convert. A dozen eggs might seem like a lot, but it's the right amount for six people.

6 servings

From the Market
Butternut squash
Kale

Spin It
1 medium acorn squash instead of butternut (leave unpeeled if desired)
4 medium Yukon Gold potatoes instead of squash, peeled
Mature spinach or Swiss chard in place of kale
2 cups thinly sliced broccoli florets and stems instead of kale

At Home
Olive oil
Salt and pepper
Mild crushed red pepper
Onion
Garlic
Eggs
Parmigiano

Spin It
2 or 3 shallots in place of onion
1 leek, white and light-green parts, instead of onion
Pecorino, Grana Padano, or mild cheddar in place of Parmigiano

½ butternut squash (halved lengthwise), peeled
3 tablespoons extra-virgin olive oil, divided
Kosher salt, freshly ground pepper
Mild crushed red pepper, such as Aleppo or gochugaru
1 small bunch kale
½ yellow onion, thinly sliced
2 garlic cloves, sliced
12 large eggs
2 ounces Parmigiano, grated, divided

Preheat oven to 300°F.

Set squash half flat side down on a cutting board and cut crosswise into thin half-moons. In a large nonstick skillet, heat 1 tablespoon oil over medium heat. Add squash, season with salt, black pepper, and a big pinch of crushed red pepper and cook, occasionally tossing gently, until squash is tender but not falling apart, about 10 minutes. Slide squash onto a large plate. Meanwhile, tear kale leaves into 2-inch pieces, then wash and spin dry.

Return skillet to medium heat. Add 1 tablespoon oil and onion. Season with salt and pepper and cook, stirring occasionally and covering pan if needed to help onion soften, until slices are very tender, completely translucent, and starting to turn light golden brown, about 8 minutes (if you rush this step, the onion will start to brown while it's still crunchy and sharp-tasting). Slide onion onto plate with squash.

Place skillet over medium-high heat and add remaining 1 tablespoon oil. Add garlic and kale and cook, tossing, until greens start to wilt, about 2 minutes. Season with salt and pepper and cook until tender, about 6 minutes.

Transfer kale to plate with onion and squash and turn off heat under skillet.

In a large bowl, whisk together eggs and half the Parmigiano until completely smooth (you can also do this in a quart container using an immersion blender). Season lightly with salt and generously with pepper. Return kale, onion, and squash to skillet and place over medium to rewarm the vegetables, about 2 minutes. Pour egg mixture into pan and fiddle around with a spatula until the vegetables are more or less evenly distributed. Scatter remaining half of Parmigiano over top.

Transfer skillet to oven and bake until surface is light golden in color and eggs are just set, about 20 minutes. Let frittata rest 5 to 10 minutes before sliding out of pan onto a cutting board or platter. Serve warm or at room temperature, cut into wedges.

BLTs with bacon-fat fried eggs

Someone told me this was known as a B.L.E.T., which is a terrible-sounding name. What's not terrible, however, is when mayo, summer tomatoes, a runny egg, chewy bacon, and kimchi juices get together for a party between two slices of bread.

4 servings

From the Market
Beefsteak tomatoes
Lettuce
Sandwich bread
Basil

Spin It
Romaine hearts,
  iceberg, or small
  green leaf lettuce
  instead of Little Gem
Any type of basil, such
  as Thai or purple,
  would be excellent
Add avocado if you
  want to

At Home
Bacon
Mayonnaise
Kimchi
Hot sauce
Eggs
Flaky sea salt
Pepper

Spin It
Pickled peppers, such
  as pepperoncini, in
  place of hot sauce

12 slices thick-cut bacon
2 large beefsteak or heirloom
  tomatoes, sliced
2 heads Little Gem lettuce, leaves
  separated
8 slices not-squishy white
  sandwich bread, such as
  Pullman, lightly toasted
Mayonnaise, kimchi, fresh basil,
  and hot sauce, for assembling
  sandwiches
4 large eggs
Flaky sea salt and freshly ground
  pepper

Preheat oven to 350°F. Line a rimmed baking sheet with foil and set a rack inside.

Arrange bacon on rack, overlapping if needed. Bake until fat is mostly rendered and bacon is crisp, 25 to 30 minutes. Reserving 2 tablespoons for cooking eggs, pour bacon fat into an airtight container and refrigerate for another day.

Arrange bacon, tomato, lettuce, toast, mayonnaise, kimchi, basil, and hot sauce on separate plates, platters, small cutting boards, and bowls so that people can help themselves. Ring the dinner bell. Then, and only then: Fry the eggs. In a large nonstick skillet, heat reserved bacon fat over medium-high heat. Add eggs and cook, shaking pan occasionally to make sure eggs slide freely, until whites are set, browned and crisp around edges but yolk is runny, about 4 minutes. Season with flaky salt and pepper and serve with other BLT fixings.

It is customary for guests to critique everyone else's sandwich-making skills and question their decisions, and to brag about how their own sandwich is the best. This behavior should be encouraged. These are big, messy sandwiches, and it would be impractical to take a bite of someone else's creation, so everyone wins.

Omelet with whipped ricotta for two

Making one big omelet and folding it in half is easy, whereas making two smaller rolled omelets is hard. Even if you nail it, one person gets stuck with a not-quite-hot omelet. I probably wouldn't mess with pea tendrils and a creamy ricotta filling on a weekday morning, but I'd serve this breakfast for dinner any night.

2 servings

From the Market
Ricotta
Pea tendrils

Spin It
Small-curd cottage cheese or cream cheese for the ricotta
Any other tender greens, such as baby kale or small watercress for the pea tendrils

At Home
Parmigiano
Salt and pepper
Eggs
Olive oil
White wine vinegar

Spin It
Cheddar, Monterey Jack, or Grana Padano can replace the Parm
Sherry vinegar or cider vinegar for the white wine vinegar

4 ounces fresh ricotta
¼ cup grated Parmigiano
Kosher salt, freshly ground pepper
6 large eggs
3 tablespoons extra-virgin olive oil, divided
2 cups pea tendrils
1 tablespoon white wine vinegar

In a small bowl, combine ricotta and Parmigiano and whisk energetically until mixture is very well blended and slightly aerated. Season with salt and pepper and set aside.

In a medium bowl, whisk eggs until very smooth and no visible streaks of egg whites remain. Season with salt and pepper. Heat a medium nonstick skillet over medium heat with 1 tablespoon olive oil. Add eggs and cook, stirring slowly in long passes across entire surface of pan and all the way around edges, until large curds form and underside is set, 1 to 2 minutes. Rap pan firmly against stovetop a few times to settle eggs into skillet. Spoon ricotta mixture across eggs, over to one side of center line. Continue to cook eggs until underside is light golden brown, about 1 minute longer. Use a spatula to lift plain half of omelet up and over the other half (as though you were folding a tortilla in half to make a taco). Slide omelet onto a cutting board.

In a medium bowl, toss pea tendrils with vinegar and remaining 2 tablespoons oil. Season with salt and pepper. Halve omelet crosswise and serve with pea tendril salad on top.

Poached egg and silky braised greens

Listen up: Swiss chard stems and ribs are a treasure—earthy, sweet, and resilient—as desirable as the ruffly leaves that surround them. Give them a head start before adding the leaves so they can soften a bit, sending vegetal juices into the pan to mingle with the garlic and olive oil. Don't balk at the amount of olive oil here, either. The leaves will melt into the saucy cooking liquid, creating a perfect soft landing for a runny egg.

2 servings

From the Market
Swiss chard

Spin It
Mature spinach or kale
for the chard

At Home
Olive oil
Garlic
Salt and pepper
Crushed red pepper
Eggs

Spin It
Sliced shallot or onion
for garlic
Pinch of cayenne or hot
smoked paprika for
crushed red pepper

1 large bunch Swiss chard,
preferably rainbow
⅓ cup extra-virgin olive oil
6 garlic cloves, smashed
Kosher salt, freshly ground pepper
½ teaspoon crushed red pepper,
plus more for serving
2 large eggs

Cut off bottommost, tough and fibrous ends of chard stems. Strip leaves off ribs, then wash and dry leaves and stems separately (be thorough, they may be coated in a fine, silty dirt). Thinly slice ribs and stems crosswise. Tear leaves into large pieces and set aside separately.

In a large skillet or Dutch oven, heat oil over medium-low heat. Add chard stems and garlic, season with salt and black pepper, and cook patiently, stirring occasionally, until stems are al dente, 8 to 10 minutes. Add crushed red pepper and chard leaves and toss to coat with oil. Season with salt and continue to cook, tossing occasionally, until leaves are bright green and very tender and stems are tender, 8 to 10 minutes more. Reduce heat to low to keep warm while you make the eggs.

In a medium saucepan, bring a few inches of water to a simmer. Crack eggs into separate small bowls, then slip into water, spacing 15 seconds apart. Cook, using a spoon to circulate water occasionally, until whites are set and yolks still runny, about 3 minutes.

Divide chard and pan sauce between two plates or shallow bowls and press a little divot into centers. Add an egg to each, season with salt, pepper, and more crushed red pepper and serve hot.

Fried grains with bacon, mushrooms, and kimchi

To make this vegetarian, omit the bacon and cook the mushrooms in two to three tablespoons olive oil to compensate for the bacon drippings. Mushrooms are porous and thirsty, and they won't sear and soften without enough fat in the pan.

2 servings

From the Market
Mushrooms
Cilantro

Spin It
Use any fresh mushrooms, such as cremini or oyster
Thinly sliced carrots, onions, or green cabbage can replace mushrooms
Scallion greens or basil instead of cilantro

At Home
Vegetable oil
Bacon
Salt
Whole grains
Kimchi
Eggs
Toasted sesame oil
Hot sauce

Spin It
Extra-virgin olive oil instead of vegetable oil
Ground pork or beef, or small peeled shrimp, instead of bacon
Water or chicken stock for kimchi liquid

7 teaspoons vegetable oil, divided, plus more if needed
2 ounces bacon, preferably thick-cut, sliced crosswise into ¾-inch pieces
8 ounces mushrooms, such as hen of the woods and/or shiitake, stems removed, caps torn
Kosher salt
2 cups cooked wheat berries, farro, or brown rice
1 cup kimchi, drained and roughly chopped, liquid reserved
Handful of chopped cilantro leaves and tender stems
2 large eggs
Toasted sesame oil and hot sauce, for serving (optional)

In a 10-inch skillet, heat 1 teaspoon oil over medium heat until just warm, less than a minute. Add bacon and cook, stirring occasionally, until starting to crisp and most of the fat has rendered, about 6 minutes. Transfer to a small plate with a slotted spoon.

Add mushrooms to drippings, increase heat to medium-high, season with salt, and toss to coat. Cook undisturbed until the mushrooms start to release some of their liquid and the undersides are browned, 3 to 4 minutes. Loosen mushrooms from pan, scraping with a wooden spoon if needed, and toss. Cook until other sides are browned and mushrooms are tender, 2 to 3 minutes more. Taste one to make sure. Transfer mushrooms to plate with bacon.

Add 1 tablespoon oil to skillet, then add grains and season with salt. If skillet looks dry or there's not enough oil to coat the grains, drizzle in more oil. Sauté grains undisturbed until starting to crisp, about 2 minutes. Toss grains, then cook undisturbed until they're more or less evenly toasted and light golden brown, but not dried out, about 2 minutes more. (Whole grains have their outer hull intact, which makes

them pleasantly chewy, but they can dry out and get tough if overcooked.)

Add kimchi and cook until it releases some juices, about 1 minute. Continue cooking until liquid evaporates and the bottom of the pan starts to brown. Remove from heat, return mushrooms and bacon to skillet with any accumulated juices, along with the reserved kimchi juice and cilantro. Toss to combine and rewarm the mushrooms and the bacon, about 30 seconds. Spoon fried grain mixture onto a platter.

Return skillet to medium-high heat and add remaining 1 tablespoon oil. Crack eggs into pan and season with salt. Cook until browned at edges, whites are set, but yolks are still runny (or not, if that's your preference), 3 to 4 minutes. Serve grains topped with fried eggs and with sesame oil and hot sauce for seasoning, if desired.

Aioli and all the things for dipping

The first time I heard of, let alone made, *le grand aïoli* was when I was in culinary school. I remember being floored by the revelation that a bowl of homemade garlic mayonnaise could anchor a glorious summer feast that you eat with your hands and share with friends. Twenty years later and it hasn't lost its appeal. I like to include a combination of raw and steamed vegetables for variety. You can keep it simple, with a few types of vegetables, eggs, and some fish, or go nuts with whatever you can get your hands on at the market.

8 to 10 servings

From the Market
Carrots
Snap peas
Green beans
Flat beans
Small potatoes
Salmon
Radishes
Lettuce
Cherry tomatoes
Cucumbers
Baguette

Spin It
Any crunchy, pretty, tasty, seasonal, good-looking vegetables can be used
Cod, hake, steelhead trout, or large shrimp for salmon

At Home
Grapeseed oil
Olive oil
Eggs
Dijon mustard
Garlic
White wine vinegar
Salt and pepper
Flaky sea salt
Lemon

Spin It
Grainy or hot mustard for Dijon

1 cup grapeseed or peanut oil
½ cup extra-virgin olive oil
1 large egg plus 1 egg yolk
1 teaspoon Dijon mustard
1 small garlic clove, finely grated
2 to 3 tablespoons white wine
　vinegar
Kosher salt, freshly ground pepper

For the platter

3 to 4 pounds mixed exquisite
　bounty of vegetables for
　steaming, such as sugar snap
　peas, haricots verts, asparagus,
　small carrots, Romano beans,
　small fingerling potatoes
　(unpeeled), cleaned and
　trimmed
12 large eggs
2 pounds skinless salmon or cod
　fillet
3 to 4 pounds mixed colorful array
　of vegetables to serve raw, such
　as baby lettuces, icicle or Easter
　Egg radishes, cherry tomatoes,
　Persian (mini) cucumbers,
　fennel, sweet bell peppers,
　celery, cleaned and trimmed
Flaky sea salt, cracked black
　pepper, lemon wedges, olive oil,
　and 2 baguettes, for serving

Make the aioli

In a measuring glass with a spout, combine oils. In a medium bowl, whisk together whole egg, egg yolk, mustard, garlic, and 2 tablespoons vinegar until completely blended. Whisking constantly, drizzle oil mixture into egg mixture drop by drop (literally), until the mixture starts to thicken and looks very smooth. This is an indication that you have an emulsion and it's safe to add the oil a little bit more quickly. Continue whisking and pouring oil in a thin stream until all of the oil has been incorporated and mayonnaise is smooth and thickened. If at any point aioli feels too thick to whisk, loosen it with a tablespoon of water and carry on. Taste and adjust seasoning with salt and pepper and more vinegar. Cover aioli and refrigerate until ready to serve.

For the platter

In a large pot fitted with a steamer basket, bring a few inches of water to a simmer. Working with one type of vegetable at a time since cooking times will vary, add vegetable to steamer basket, cover, and cook until crisp-tender: 2 minutes for sugar snap peas; 3 minutes for green beans, wax beans, and asparagus; 5 minutes for carrots and Romano beans; and 10 to 12 minutes for small whole potatoes. Transfer vegetables to at least two large rimmed baking sheets lined with paper towels to cool as they are done. Top off water in pot as needed between batches. When cool, cover vegetables with damp paper towels and then a layer of plastic wrap; refrigerate for up to 3 hours.

With water at a simmer, place eggs in steamer, cover, and cook 8 minutes for hard-boiled eggs with tender whites and creamy, gently set yolks. Plunge into a bowl of ice water to cool. Drain eggs and refrigerate until ready to serve.

Season the salmon with kosher salt and freshly ground pepper, place in steamer basket, and cook until just opaque at the center, 6 to 8 minutes. Let cool, then cover loosely with plastic wrap and refrigerate for up to 3 hours.

Meanwhile, prep the raw vegetables. Separate adorable baby lettuce leaves, then wash and spin dry. Leave small radishes and baby white turnips whole, with good-looking tops attached (or trimmed, if you prefer). Slice larger radishes into ½-inch wedges or thin rounds. Halve tomatoes and small cucumbers. Cut fennel, sweet bell peppers, and celery into thin spears. Cover and chill.

To serve, arrange vegetables and salmon on a large platter or platters and tuck lemon wedges around edge. Divide aioli among three or four bowls with spoons, and set out for passing. Peel and halve the eggs and season with flaky salt and cracked pepper; arrange on platters. Squeeze some lemon juice over everything and drizzle with oil; season with flaky salt and cracked pepper and serve with baguettes.

Carbonara stracciatella

Every time you grate a wedge of Parmigiano down to the rind, save the rind. I keep a zip-top bag in my freezer specifically for this purpose and make regular deposits. When I've got a nice stash, it's time to make Parm broth. It's awesome in braises and tomato sauces, or add it to the cooking liquid for beans or grains. Or, make this carbonara-inspired stracciatella (Italian for egg-drop soup), which gets a little lightness from barely wilted greens. Hot tip: If you can't wait, most cheese shops will sell you the rinds.

4 servings

From the Market
Lettuce

Spin It
Any tender lettuce, spring greens, mature arugula, or inner leaves from a head of escarole can be used

At Home
Parmigiano and Parmigiano rinds
Bay leaf and/or parsley
Salt and pepper
Bacon
Eggs

Spin It
Grana Padano instead of Parmigiano
Pancetta or guanciale instead of bacon, or omit

For the Parmigiano broth
8 ounces Parmigiano rinds
1 bay leaf and/or handful of parsley sprigs
Freshly ground pepper
Kosher salt

For the soup
12 ounces bacon, preferably thick-cut
4 large eggs
½ cup grated Parmigiano, divided
Kosher salt
6 cups tender lettuce, cut into 1½-inch-thick pieces
Freshly ground pepper

Make the Parmigiano broth
In a stockpot, combine rinds, bay leaf, and 2 quarts water. Bring to a simmer over medium-high heat, stirring often, then reduce to a gentle simmer and cook until broth is infused with Parm flavor without being too salty or cloying, about 45 minutes. Make sure to stir every 10 minutes or so to prevent the rinds from sticking to the bottom. (Some will stick no matter what; steel wool is the best way to clean the pot.)

Pour broth through a fine-mesh sieve into a large bowl or measuring cup and let cool; you should have a scant 2 quarts. (If desired, cover and chill for up to 5 days, or freeze for up to 3 months.)

Use a soup spoon to skim fat off surface of broth (if chilled, fat will solidify and lift off easily). Pour broth into a medium saucepan and season with many grinds of pepper. Heat over medium until lightly simmering, then cook 5 minutes to meld flavors. Taste and adjust seasoning with salt (go light; the bacon and the grated Parmigiano are both salty). Keep hot over low heat.

Make the soup
Meanwhile, in a large skillet, cook bacon over medium heat, turning occasionally, until crisp, about 8 minutes. Drain on paper towels, then cut crosswise into 1-inch pieces.

In a bowl, whisk eggs with half the Parmigiano and season with salt. Bring broth back to a simmer over medium-high heat and use a whisk to stir vigorously in big circles until a vortex forms in center. Without stirring, stream in eggs and let sit 1 to 2 minutes to gently set.

Divide lettuce among bowls. Ladle stracciatella over lettuce and top with bacon, remaining Parmigiano, and more black pepper.

Pasta and Grains

If you've been thinking of pasta as a simple starch, rejoice! It's made from wheat, which means it can claim fellowship among grainy salads, hearty granolas, and health-halo pancakes, too.

Pasta all'amatriciana with confit tomatoes	135
Spaghetti with quick-braised artichoke hearts	136
Pasta with cauliflower, sausage, and big bread crumbs	140
Spaghetti aglio e olio with all-o the parsley	143
Caprese mac and cheese	144
Lobster pasta with grated tomato sauce	147
Fregola with clams, corn, and basil pesto	148
Greek-ish grain salad	151
Grains and roasted squash with spicy buttermilk dressing	152
Pomegranate-parsley tabbouleh	155
No-stir maple granola	156
Cosmo's power pancakes	159

Pasta all'amatriciana with confit tomatoes

This recipe exists because of a tray of tomato confit that was left over from a day during the photo shoot. Susie Theodorou, the gold-medal food stylist who beautified my recipes, kept pressing me to come up with a dish for them. One thing led to another, and twenty minutes later, we were taking photos of this pasta dish, which was our dinner that night. If you don't have confited tomatoes on hand, simply use canned tomatoes and olive oil instead.

4 servings

From the Market
Pancetta

Spin It
Slab bacon or guanciale
   for the pancetta

At Home
Salt and pepper
8 confited tomatoes
Red onion
Crushed red pepper
Long fusilli
Parmigiano

Spin It
Spaghetti would be
   a classic pasta
   substitution, or
   use bucatini,
   perciatelli, regular
   fusilli, or rigatoni

Kosher salt
4 ounces pancetta (uncut)
2 tablespoons confit tomato oil
   (from confited tomatoes) or
   ¼ cup extra-virgin olive oil
1 red onion, quartered, thinly
   sliced
Freshly ground pepper
8 confited tomatoes (see page 63
   for method), or 8 whole peeled
   tomatoes from a 28-ounce can
1 teaspoon crushed red pepper,
   plus more for serving
1 pound long fusilli (fusilli
   lunghi)
Grated Parmigiano, for serving

Bring a large pot of salted water to a boil for pasta.

Cut pancetta into 1 × ½-inch pieces and put in a Dutch oven, then place over medium-low heat. Cook, stirring occasionally, until about half the fat has rendered and edges are starting to turn golden brown and pieces are equal parts crisp and chewy, 8 to 10 minutes. Use a slotted spoon to transfer pancetta to a small plate and set aside. Reserve pot with drippings.

Add confit oil to pot, increase heat to medium, then stir in onion and season with salt and black pepper. Cook, stirring every couple of minutes, until onion is translucent and floppy, 6 to 8 minutes. Don't rush this step; it's essential for unlocking the onion's sweetness. Increase heat to medium-high and cook until onion is golden brown, 3 to 4 minutes longer.

Meanwhile, tear tomatoes into ½-inch-thick pieces.

Add tomatoes and crushed red pepper to pot and cook, stirring often, until tomatoes give up their juices and start to lightly caramelize. Stir pancetta back into sauce along with any accumulated juices, then taste and adjust seasoning with salt and black pepper. Remove from heat and cover pot until pasta is ready.

Add pasta to boiling water and set a timer for 2 to 3 minutes less than package instructions (it should be very al dente and will finish cooking in the sauce). Use tongs or a spider to transfer pasta directly to pot of sauce along with about ½ cup pasta water. Cook over medium high, stirring and tossing constantly with tongs and adding ¼ cupfuls of pasta water as needed until pasta is al dente and coated in a glossy, luscious sauce, about 2 minutes.

Serve topped with Parmigiano and more crushed red pepper, if you like.

Spaghetti with quick-braised artichoke hearts

Artichokes are the bogeyman of the vegetable world, and their tiny cat-claw thorns are as terrifying as cobra fangs. No wonder: We've been coddled into buying pre-cut squash, clementines that peel themselves, and zucchini in "zoodle" form. People! Reclaim your ancient power. Hold a squeaky, dense, dangerous artichoke in your hand and sculpt it down to its silky, meaty little innards and meditate on what a weird vegetable you're dealing with. And then: Eat pasta.

4 servings

From the Market
Artichokes
Parsley

Spin It
This is an aglio e olio sauce with artichokes cooked into it. The same process will work with roughly 2 cups chopped broccoli, cauliflower, thin green beans, or diced butternut squash instead of the artichokes.

At Home
Lemon
Salt and pepper
Garlic
Olive oil
White wine
Spaghetti
Crushed red pepper
Parmigiano

Spin It
Any other long pasta can be used, such as bucatini or linguine, or use a large tube like paccheri

2 lemons, halved
3 large artichokes
Kosher salt
10 garlic cloves (about 1 head),
    smashed
⅓ cup extra-virgin olive oil
Freshly ground pepper
½ cup roughly chopped parsley
    leaves
⅓ cup white wine
1 pound spaghetti
Crushed red pepper and grated
    Parmigiano, for serving

Fill a large bowl with cold water, squeeze in juice from 2 lemon halves, then drop squeezed-out halves into water. This is acidulated water, and it will prevent the artichokes from oxidizing and turning brown as they soak.

Working with one artichoke at a time, use a serrated knife to trim stem, leaving as much of it intact as possible (it's all edible). Rub cut end with a lemon half. Snap off outermost leaves, then use knife to cut off top two-thirds of pointed end, exposing fuzzy choke. If choke is not visible, slice off ½-inch-thick slices until it reveals itself. Rub cut edges with lemon. Working your way around, continue to snap off leaves until you get down to the tender, pale green-yellow ones. Use a paring knife to shave off the rough bits where the leaves were attached to base, then use a vegetable peeler to peel the stem to expose the light green layer. Rub lemon all over the stem.

You'll now be holding a coupe-shaped artichoke, with the heart and trimmed inner leaves perched atop a length of stem. See! Not so hard. Cut artichoke lengthwise into quarters, or sixths if large, then use a paring knife to cut out choke (the bristly fine leaves that sit on top of the saucer-shaped heart). Drop trimmed quarters into lemon water and repeat with remaining artichokes. This takes way longer to describe than it does to do in real life.

Bring a large pot of salted water to a boil for the pasta.

Place garlic in a deep, wide skillet or small Dutch oven and add oil. Place over medium heat and cook, stirring occasionally, until oil is sizzling around garlic, about 2 minutes. Season with a big pinch of salt and many cranks of black pepper and cook, using a spoon to break garlic into smaller pieces, until it is pale golden and very fragrant, about 3 minutes.

Lift out artichoke pieces and shake off excess water. Carefully add to pan with oil and garlic; the liquid may sputter, so watch your wrists. Add half of the parsley, season with salt, and stir to coat with oil. Cook until artichokes are vibrant green, about 2 minutes. Add wine, increase heat to medium-high, and simmer until wine is reduced by half. Cover, reduce heat to medium, and cook until a cake tester slides easily into thickest part of artichoke, about 5 minutes.

Add spaghetti to the boiling water and set a timer for 2 to 3 minutes less than package instructions (it should be very al dente and will finish cooking in the sauce).

Using a mesh spider or tongs, transfer spaghetti directly to artichoke mixture (still over medium heat). Gently toss pasta into sauce, adding splashes of pasta water as needed to generously coat spaghetti. Simmer, tossing constantly but without breaking artichokes into pieces, until it looks plenty saucy in bottom of pan, 2 to 3 minutes. Add remaining parsley and squeeze in juice from remaining lemon half and toss to combine. Serve pasta with crushed red pepper and Parmigiano.

Pasta with cauliflower, sausage, and big bread crumbs

If you've had orecchiette with broccoli and sausage, you can imagine what this tastes like. Because cauliflower is sweeter than broccoli, I usually choose hot sausage for contrast. I'm pretty into the starch-on-starch boldness of serving coarse lemony bread crumbs on top of chewy pasta; use day-old or days-old bread, torn from the inside of the loaf.

4 to 6 servings

From the Market
Parsley
Italian sausage
Cauliflower

Spin It
½ pound bacon can replace the sausage
If using sausage links, remove casings before cooking
Broccoli, Romanesco, or halved Brussels sprouts for the cauliflower

At Home
Salt and pepper
Butter
Day-old bread
Lemon
Olive oil
Garlic
Pasta
Parmigiano

Spin It
Panko can be used instead of fresh crumbs; toast in same way

Kosher salt, freshly ground pepper
4 tablespoons (2 ounces) unsalted butter
2 cups coarse torn bread crumbs (¼-inch pieces)
Grated zest of 1 lemon
¼ cup finely chopped fresh parsley
3 tablespoons extra-virgin olive oil
1 pound hot and/or sweet Italian sausage meat
5 garlic cloves, thinly sliced
1 pound cauliflower, cut into bite-size pieces
1 pound rigatoni or orecchiette
¼ cup grated Parmigiano, plus more for serving
3 tablespoons lemon juice

Bring a large pot of salted water to a boil for the pasta.

In a large skillet, melt butter over medium heat until foaming. Add torn bread, season with salt and pepper, and cook, tossing, until golden brown and toasted, 4 to 5 minutes. Transfer bread crumbs to a medium bowl or plate, add lemon zest and parsley, and toss to combine.

Wipe out skillet and return to medium-high heat. Add olive oil and when shimmering, add sausage. Use a wooden spoon to break into 1- to 2-inch pieces, and cook undisturbed until dark golden brown on underside, 5 to 7 minutes. Use the spoon to scrape up sausage, then toss quickly to get a little heat on all sides. Use a slotted spoon to transfer to a plate. Add garlic to drippings in pan, remove from heat, and stir to coat (there should be enough residual heat to soften the garlic almost immediately). Set skillet aside.

Add cauliflower to boiling water and cook until tender all the way through but not mushy, 4 to 6 minutes. Use a slotted spoon or mesh spider to transfer to skillet with garlic and stir to coat with oil.

Add pasta to same pot of boiling water and set a timer for 2 to 3 minutes less than package instructions (it should be very al dente and will finish cooking in the sauce). Use a slotted spoon or spider to transfer pasta to skillet with cauliflower. Add browned sausage and return skillet to medium heat. Cook, tossing and adding spoonfuls of pasta water into mixture, until pan sauce starts to cling to noodles. Add Parmigiano and continue to cook, tossing and moistening with pasta water as needed, until cheese is melted and pan sauce is glossy and abundant. Add lemon juice and half of reserved bread crumbs and toss to combine. Serve pasta with remaining bread crumbs on top and more Parmigiano on the side.

Spaghetti aglio e olio with all-o the parsley

Even when there is nothing to eat, there is always spaghetti aglio e olio. There's lots of parsley in this version—maybe enough to convince yourself you're getting a serving of greens. Keep this dish in mind when you're staring down a bunch of herbs in the crisper drawer.

4 servings

From the Market
Parsley

Spin It
Basil would lend more aromatic, sweeter notes and can replace part or all of the parsley
½ cup chives in place of parsley would amplify the garlicky and pungent flavors

At Home
Salt and pepper
Spaghetti
Olive oil
Garlic
Anchovy fillets
Crushed red pepper
Parmigiano

Spin It
Any other long pasta, such as bucatini or linguine, can replace the spaghetti

---

Kosher salt, freshly ground pepper
1 pound spaghetti
⅓ cup extra-virgin olive oil
10 garlic cloves, smashed
2 oil-packed anchovy fillets (optional)
½ teaspoon crushed red pepper, plus more for serving
1 cup lightly packed chopped fresh parsley leaves and tender stems
Parmigiano, for serving

Bring a large pot of salted water to a boil for pasta. Add pasta and set a timer for 2 to 3 minutes less than package instructions (it should be very al dente and will finish cooking in the sauce).

Meanwhile, in a large skillet or Dutch oven, heat oil and garlic over medium heat, stirring occasionally, until bubbles appear and garlic is starting to turn translucent, 2 to 3 minutes. Season garlic with salt and pepper (I like a lot of pepper, and I like how its flavor opens up in the oil). Continue cooking, breaking garlic into smaller pieces with the edge of a wooden spoon, until golden brown and softened, 3 to 4 minutes more. Add anchovies (if using) and crushed red pepper and stir until anchovies disintegrate, about 1 minute. If pasta is not yet done, slide skillet off heat.

Scoop out a cup of pasta cooking liquid, then drain spaghetti and transfer to skillet along with ½ cup pasta water. Bring to a simmer over medium heat, add parsley, and cook, tossing constantly with tongs and adding more pasta water as needed, until pasta is al dente and sauce is just thick enough to coat pasta but there's still plenty of extra sauce in skillet, 2 to 3 minutes.

Serve with more crushed red pepper and Parmigiano for grating over.

Caprese mac and cheese

You probably didn't think you needed a mac and cheese for summer months. Surprise! This is a nostalgic take on a room-temperature, portable pasta my mom used to make every August when I was a teenager: She'd toss together marinated tomatoes, milky fresh mozzarella, and basil with just-drained pasta that would melt the cheese on contact. My version is baked, but the way it tastes takes me back to those summers.

6 servings

From the Market
Ricotta
Heavy cream
Basil
Cherry tomatoes
Mozzarella

Spin It
Small-curd, whole-milk cottage cheese can replace the ricotta
¼ cup prepared pesto can be substituted for the basil
2 cups roughly chopped tomatoes instead of cherry tomatoes
For another cheesy note, add ½ cup grated Parmigiano to the cream mixture

At Home
Salt and pepper
Shell pasta
Garlic
Olive oil
Crushed red pepper

Spin It
Any large pasta with deep grooves, such as lumaconi or cavatappi, for the shells

---

Kosher salt, freshly ground pepper
1 cup whole-milk ricotta
½ cup heavy cream
1 cup finely chopped fresh basil leaves
1 pound large shell pasta
4 garlic cloves, smashed
12 ounces cherry tomatoes (any type), halved
12 ounces salted fresh mozzarella, torn into ½-inch pieces
Extra-virgin olive oil, for drizzling
Crushed red pepper, for serving

Preheat oven to 375°F.

Bring a large pot of water to a boil and season it generously with salt.

In a large bowl, combine the ricotta, cream, and basil and whisk until smooth. Season generously with salt and pepper. Set aside.

Cook pasta in boiling water for 2 to 3 minutes less than package instructions (undercooking the pasta is key so that it is al dente, not mushy, when baked). Use a mesh spider or slotted spoon to transfer pasta straight into bowl with ricotta mixture and stir until pasta is evenly coated (reserve pasta pot with water). Taste pasta and season with salt and pepper, if needed. Let cool for a few minutes, tossing occasionally.

Meanwhile, simmer garlic in reserved pasta water until completely tender, 3 to 4 minutes. Reserve a cup of pasta liquid, then drain garlic, transfer to a cutting board, and finely chop.

Add garlic to pasta mixture, along with tomatoes and half of mozzarella (eyeball it); toss well to combine. Scrape this whole pasta party into a 3-quart baking dish, drizzle reserved pasta water over, and top with remaining mozzarella.

Bake until cheese is softened and melty, but not browned, about 20 minutes. Let pasta cool 10 minutes before serving. Drizzle with olive oil and season with salt, black pepper, and crushed red pepper. It may look a little dry on top, but it will be saucy and delightful down below, so make sure to spoon up servings from the bottom of the dish.

Lobster pasta with grated tomato sauce

Credit for this genius grated tomato method, which turns the flesh into pulp and removes the skin, goes to chef Ashley Christensen, who shared it with *Bon Appétit* in 2016. Because the tomato is halfway to sauce when it hits the pan, it barely has to cook, yielding a fresh, aromatic, sunny flavor. It's even good without the lobster (but have it with the lobster).

2 servings

From the Market
Live lobster
Beefsteak tomatoes
Basil

Spin It
1 pound large peeled and deveined shrimp, for lobster
2 cups cherry tomatoes, halved (do not grate), instead of beefsteaks
Large heirloom tomatoes for beefsteaks

At Home
Butter
Garlic
Salt and pepper
Spaghetti
Olive oil

Spin It
You could replace the butter with olive oil, or use a mix
Bucatini or linguine instead of spaghetti

---

1 (1¼-pound) live lobster
Kosher salt, freshly ground pepper
3 large beefsteak tomatoes (2 pounds)
4 tablespoons (2 ounces) unsalted butter
4 garlic cloves, thinly sliced
Handful of basil leaves, torn
8 ounces spaghetti or thick spaghetti
Extra-virgin olive oil, for drizzling

In a large pot fitted with a steamer basket, bring 2 inches of water to a simmer over medium-high heat. Add lobster, cover, and steam for 8 minutes (lobster will not be quite cooked through). Place lobster in a colander and rinse under cold running water to stop the cooking. Crack shells and remove meat from tails, claws, and knuckles. Cut tail meat into bite-size pieces; leave claws and knuckles intact. Cover picked lobster meat with a sheet of plastic wrap and set aside.

Rinse out pot, fill with water for cooking pasta, salt it generously, and bring to a boil over high heat.

Cut a thin slice off base of each tomato. Hold tomato at stem end and use large holes of a box grater to grate flesh and pulp into a large bowl. The skin should unfurl as you go, until you're left with just the stem and shredded skin in your hand (which you can discard). Some skin might pass through, and that's fine, too.

In a large skillet, combine butter and garlic, place over medium heat and cook, stirring occasionally until butter is foaming and garlic is translucent and very fragrant, about 2 minutes. Add grated tomato and season with salt and pepper. Simmer until sauce is slightly thickened, about 10 minutes. Add basil, stir to combine, then remove from heat.

Add pasta to boiling water and set a timer for 2 to 3 minutes less than package instructions (it should be very al dente and will finish cooking in the sauce).

Return sauce to a simmer over medium heat and use a mesh spider or tongs to transfer pasta directly into pan with sauce. Cook pasta and sauce, adding splashes of pasta cooking liquid and tossing constantly, until noodles are al dente and sauce is glossy and thick enough to coat pasta, 2 to 3 minutes. Add lobster to sauce, toss to combine, and cook just until lobster is warmed through, about 2 minutes (it will be rubbery and dry if it overcooks, and you will not be happy).

Divide pasta between two bowls and top each portion with a claw. Serve drizzled with a little olive oil.

Fregola with clams, corn, and basil pesto

Fregola is a Sardinian bead-shaped toasted pasta with a rough surface, chewy texture, and slightly smoky flavor. Rustichella d'Abruzzo is my favorite domestically available brand of fregola; you can find it online. Fregola and clams is a pretty classic combo—I added the corn because it's about the same size as the fregola, and because clams and corn feel like summer to me.

4 to 6 servings

From the Market
Basil
Shallots
Clams
Fregola
Corn

Spin It
Add a pint of cherry tomatoes to the pot when you put in the clams
Substitute parsley or chives for one-quarter of the basil
Substitute mussels for half the clams
Use mezze rigatoni, orecchiette, or ditalini instead of fregola

At Home
Garlic
Parmigiano
Olive oil
Lemon
Salt and pepper
Butter
White wine

Spin It
Use water in place of white wine and add a tablespoon of lemon juice to the pan sauce

For the pesto
½ garlic clove, finely grated
¼ cup grated Parmigiano
1 cup packed fresh basil leaves (stems reserved)
3 tablespoons extra-virgin olive oil
Finely grated zest of ½ lemon
Kosher salt, freshly ground pepper

For the clams and fregola
Kosher salt
2 tablespoons unsalted butter
2 tablespoons extra-virgin olive oil
3 garlic cloves, thinly sliced
2 small shallots, thinly sliced
½ cup white wine
24 littleneck or Manila clams, scrubbed
12 ounces fregola
2 cups corn kernels (from 3 to 4 ears)

Make the pesto
In a blender or food processor, combine garlic, Parmigiano, basil, and oil and blend until very smooth, scraping down sides as needed and adding a tablespoon or two of water if needed to get things moving. Add lemon zest and season with salt and pepper. Set pesto aside (you should have about ½ cup).

Cook the clams and fregola
Bring a large pot of water to a boil for the fregola and season it generously with salt. In a medium Dutch oven or large cast-iron skillet, heat butter and oil over medium-high heat. When butter is foaming, add garlic, shallots, and reserved basil stems and cook until mixture is fragrant, about 2 minutes. Add wine and bring to a simmer. Add clams, toss to coat, cover, and cook, checking and stirring every few minutes, until clams begin to open,

3 to 5 minutes. As clams open, transfer them with a slotted spoon to a medium bowl, but try to keep pot covered as much as possible. Fish out basil stems and keep pan sauce warm over very low heat. (If you want a shell-free dining experience, gently liberate clams from their shells and return them to bowl with a splash or two of pasta water over them so they don't dry out.)

Cook fregola until 1 or 2 minutes shy of al dente. Scoop 1 cup of pasta water into pan with clam sauce. Drain fregola and add to sauce along with half of the pesto. Add corn and bring mixture to a simmer. Cook, stirring, until liquid starts to thicken and fregola is al dente, about 2 minutes. Add clams and any accumulated liquid from bowl. Cook, stirring and tossing, until clams are warmed through, 2 minutes. Serve fregola and clams topped with more pesto.

Greek-ish grain salad

I love grain salads, and I love Greek salad, and there's not much in this world that isn't improved by a few slabs of feta cheese. Given all that, I'm not sure why it took me so long to put them all together. This is the big salad of my dreams.

4 to 6 servings

From the Market
Scallions
Chile
English cucumber
Olives
Feta
Romaine
Mint

Spin It
½ red onion, cut into thin half-moons, instead of scallions
Use ½ to 1 teaspoon crushed red pepper in place of fresh chile
If you like kalamata olives, use them
Ricotta salata or Cotija can replace the feta
Any crisp lettuce can replace the romaine

At Home
Salt
Farro
Red wine vinegar
Anchovy fillets
Olive oil

Spin It
Use any whole grain you like in place of farro; cook times will vary

Soaked? Stoked!

Whole grains and dried beans both benefit greatly from an overnight or all-day soak, so whenever you can plan ahead, cover them in cold water and let them hydrate. Soaked grains and beans cook faster and more evenly, which is reason enough to do it. The process also activates enzymes that make grains and beans easier to digest.

2 tablespoons kosher salt, plus more for seasoning
1 cup farro, soaked overnight if possible (see note)
2 bunches scallions, trimmed, sliced into thin rounds
1 fresh red medium-spicy chile, such as Fresno, thinly sliced into rounds
¼ cup red wine vinegar
2 oil-packed anchovy fillets, finely chopped
1 English hothouse cucumber, roughly chopped
4 ounces black Cerignola olives, smashed, pits removed
⅓ cup extra-virgin olive oil
6 ounces feta, cut into ½-inch-thick slabs
Freshly ground pepper
1 romaine heart, leaves cut crosswise into strips
1 cup fresh mint leaves

Bring 4 quarts water to a boil over high heat and add 2 tablespoons salt. Add farro, reduce heat to a brisk simmer, and cook until al dente, 20 minutes if soaked, 30 minutes if not. Drain farro and spread out on a small rimmed baking sheet or platter to cool.

Meanwhile, in a large bowl, combine scallions, chile, and vinegar and season with a 4-finger pinch of salt. Stir to combine and let sit 10 minutes for flavors to meld.

Add farro to bowl with the scallion mixture, along with anchovies, cucumber, and olives. Toss to coat, then add olive oil and feta and gently fold together. Taste and season with salt and pepper.

Just before serving, add romaine and mint and toss gently to combine.

Grains and roasted squash with spicy buttermilk dressing

The base of this dish can be made with any whole grain, and you can use any vegetable that roasts well instead of the squash. In the fall and winter I do this with cauliflower steaks, thin cabbage wedges, and sweet potatoes that have been cut into planks. In the spring, it's carrots, radishes, and baby turnips. In summer I'll use thick slices of eggplant for the job, or I might grill wedges of romaine (instead of roasting). Fresh beefsteak tomatoes would be amazing, too—as long as you leave them raw.

6 servings

From the Market
Honeynut squash
Tender herbs

Spin It
Use any winter
  squash you like (see
  headnote for other
  vegetable options)
Lettuces, such as Little
  Gem or endive, for
  herbs
Basil, chives, tarragon,
  dill, and/or mint can
  be used

At Home
Wheat berries
Salt and pepper
Olive oil
Yogurt
Buttermilk
Crushed Calabrian
  chiles in oil
Lemon

Spin It
Sambal or sriracha for
  Calabrian chiles
Cider vinegar or
  rice vinegar for
  lemon juice
Any whole grain can be
  substituted for wheat
  berries

---

1 cup wheat berries, soaked
  overnight if possible
  (see note, page 151)
Kosher salt
2 Honeynut or 1 butternut squash,
  scrubbed
2 tablespoons extra-virgin olive oil
Freshly ground pepper
½ cup plain whole-milk yogurt
½ cup buttermilk
1 teaspoon crushed Calabrian
  chiles in oil
1 lemon, halved
1 cup chopped tender herbs and/
  or fennel stems and fronds

Cook the wheat berries like pasta, in a big pot of salted boiling water, until tender, 20 minutes if soaked, 30 to 40 if not (start checking at around the 20-minute mark).

Meanwhile, preheat oven to 450°F.

Peel the squash if desired (the thin skins are edible). Halve squash crosswise at the spot where the neck and the bulb meet. Cut neck crosswise into ¾-inch-thick rounds. Halve bulb end, scoop out seeds, and cut squash into 1-inch-thick half-moons. Transfer all of the squash to a rimmed baking sheet, drizzle with oil, season with salt and pepper, and toss to coat. Spread the squash out and roast until tender and lightly browned, 20 to 30 minutes, tossing gently half-way through.

Meanwhile, make the dressing: In a small bowl, stir together yogurt and buttermilk until combined, then taste and season with salt and pepper. Add Calabrian chiles and swirl together. Taste and season with salt and juice of ½ lemon. Thin with a splash of water if it doesn't seem loose enough to be described as "dressing" (especially relevant if using Greek yogurt).

Drain wheat berries and transfer to a medium bowl. Let cool until warm, tossing occasionally. Stir in half of the dressing.

Spread out the dressed grains on a serving platter. Top with squash and drizzle remaining dressing over. Toss herbs in a small bowl with juice of remaining ½ lemon. Season with salt. Scatter herbs over.

Pomegranate-parsley tabbouleh

I chose freekeh for this nonconventional tabbouleh because I love its smoky, slightly lemony flavor, which is amplified by the sour-sweet pomegranates and punchy dressing. This salad is more herbs than anything else—make it when you have a glut of parsley on hand. It's a great foil for meaty braises, roasts, and slow-cooked fatty proteins like short ribs or the lamb shoulder on page 216.

6 servings

From the Market
Shallot
Serrano chile
Sumac
Pomegranates
Parsley
Fennel
Mint

At Home
Freekeh
Salt and pepper
Ginger
Olive oil
Lime
Maple syrup
Flaky sea salt

Spin It
3 or 4 scallions instead of shallot
Jalapeño or red Fresno chile instead of a serrano
Zest of 1 lime for sumac
2 pints fresh red currants for the pomegranates
1 celery heart with tender leaves instead of fennel
Cilantro or chives instead of mint

Spin It
Bulgur, unhulled barley, or semi-pearled farro instead of freekeh
Pomegranate molasses instead of maple syrup

---

1 cup freekeh
Kosher salt, freshly ground pepper
1 small shallot, finely chopped
1 small serrano chile, finely grated
1-inch piece fresh ginger, peeled, finely grated
½ cup extra-virgin olive oil, plus more for serving
¼ cup fresh lime juice
1 teaspoon maple syrup
2 teaspoons sumac, plus more for serving
2 pomegranates
1 big bunch parsley, leaves and tender stems very roughly chopped
Small fennel bulb, stalks and bulb thinly sliced, fronds set aside
Handful of mint, leaves torn if large
Flaky sea salt, for serving

Cook freekeh in a large pot of boiling salted water until al dente, 15 to 20 minutes. Drain and transfer to a rimmed baking sheet; season while warm with salt and pepper. Set aside.

Meanwhile, in a small bowl, make the dressing. Combine shallot, serrano, ginger, olive oil, lime juice, maple syrup, and sumac. Taste and season with salt. Let lime dressing sit 10 minutes to develop flavors.

Cut pomegranates in half. Working over a large bowl with one half at a time, hold pomegranate cut side down in your palm with your fingers stretched wide. Use a large wooden spoon to forcefully and repeatedly smack pomegranate skin, which will send the seeds raining down into the bowl. Repeat with remaining pomegranate halves. Fill bowl with cold water to cover pomegranate. Any little bits of pith that were dislodged will float to surface; skim them off, then drain seeds and shake off excess liquid.

In a serving bowl, toss together parsley, fennel, fennel fronds, and mint. Add cooled freekeh, season with salt, and toss gently to combine. Add lime dressing and toss with your hands to thoroughly coat ingredients. Add pomegranate seeds and toss gently to disperse them. Drizzle lightly with olive oil and sprinkle some flaky sea salt and sumac over.

No-stir maple granola

Shout-out to granola kingpin and recreational weather commentator Nekisia Davis, who did the world a favor by inventing Early Bird Granola. I'm one of many imitators who have tried to hack her groundbreaking salty-sweet olive oil–enriched formula, which to this day has no equal. Most granola recipes advise you to stir every 10 to 20 minutes to ensure even browning, but when I do that I fling oats and nuts all over my oven's floor and/or burn a knuckle. Out of sheer laziness, I wondered if I could make granola without unleashing chaos. This is that.

Makes about 2 quarts

At Home
Rolled oats
Seeds and nuts
Coconut flakes
Olive oil
Maple syrup
Salt
Cardamom
Dried fruit

Spin It
Kamut flakes for oats
Any combination of seeds such as sunflower, pepitas, sesame seeds, and/or hemp seeds
¼ cup cacao nibs to replace equivalent amount of seeds
Nuts such as pistachio, pecan, walnut, almond, and cashew
Additional coconut flakes can be used to replace some nuts or seeds
Cinnamon or nutmeg for the cardamom
Dried fruit such as dates, apricots, sour cherries, gooseberries, and/or golden raisins

---

3 cups rolled oats (not quick-cooking)
2 cups seeds and/or raw nuts
1 cup unsweetened coconut flakes
½ cup extra-virgin olive oil
½ cup pure maple syrup
2 teaspoons kosher salt
1 teaspoon ground cardamom
1½ cups mixed dried fruit

Position a rack in center of oven and preheat to 350°F.

In a large bowl, toss together oats, seeds, and coconut flakes to combine. Add oil and maple syrup and use a spatula to fold mixture together until everything is evenly coated. Add salt and cardamom and stir through.

Scrape granola mixture onto a large rimmed baking sheet and use a spatula to spread it into an even layer, wall to wall. Bake, rotating sheet back to front halfway through, until nuts and oats visible on top are very dark golden and mixture is fragrant and toasty, about 35 minutes.

Meanwhile, cut dried fruit into smallish pieces—I use a pair of kitchen shears.

As soon as granola comes out of oven, add fruit to baking sheet and toss to disperse evenly; the fruit will soften and pick up seasoning. Let granola cool completely on sheet, then transfer to airtight containers and store at room temperature. It will keep well for up to 3 weeks.

Cosmo's power pancakes

I have made these hundreds of times for my younger son, Cosmo, who loves pancakes like Garfield loves lasagna. Rather than coming up with reasons to deny him, I found ways to add nutritional value to a buttermilk pancake recipe from *Bon Appétit* that he loved. I reduced the sugar, added whole wheat flour, and tossed in oats and seeds. As long as there was maple syrup on the table, he was happy. Make the whole recipe. Extras can be refrigerated in an airtight container or zip-top bag for a day or two, and reheated in the toaster.

Makes 12 (3-inch) pancakes

At Home
Buttermilk
Chia seeds
All-purpose flour
Whole wheat flour
Rolled oats
Flaxseed meal
Sugar
Baking powder
Baking soda
Salt
Eggs
Butter
Maple syrup
 and/or jam

Spin It
½ cup plain yogurt stirred into 1 cup cow's milk or nut milk for the buttermilk
Use at least ½ cup all-purpose flour and enough whole wheat flour to measure 1½ cups total
Unsweetened coconut flakes for the oats
Hemp seeds or cooked quinoa to replace the flaxseed meal
Ghee, coconut oil, or bacon fat for the butter

1½ cups buttermilk, shaken
⅓ cup chia seeds
¾ cup all-purpose flour (spooned and leveled)
¾ cup whole wheat flour
⅓ cup rolled oats (not quick-cooking)
2 tablespoons flaxseed meal
1 tablespoon sugar
1 teaspoon baking powder
1 teaspoon baking soda
½ teaspoon kosher salt
2 large eggs, whisked to blend
2 tablespoons unsalted butter, melted, plus more for greasing
Butter, pure maple syrup, and/or jam, for serving

Preheat a griddle to 375°F, or place a heavy skillet, preferably cast-iron, over medium/medium-high heat.

In a measuring cup with a spout, stir together buttermilk and chia seeds until seeds are coated and nothing is stuck to bottom of cup.

In a medium bowl, whisk or toss together both flours, oats, flaxseed meal, sugar, baking powder, baking soda, and salt to combine.

Pour buttermilk-chia mixture, eggs, and 2 tablespoons melted butter into dry ingredients and fold with a rubber spatula or a wooden spoon just until batter is combined with no dry ingredients visible (some lumps are okay).

Lightly grease griddle with butter. Spoon batter onto the griddle in roughly 3-inch rounds and cook until a few bubbles appear and break on surface, and top of batter looks slightly matte, about 4 minutes. Turn and cook on second side for 1 to 2 minutes longer (these can be any size; cook time will vary, so heed the visual cues instead of the clock). If you're not sure if the pancakes are done, tear one open to inspect it, and then reward yourself by eating it. This is your right and privilege as the cook.

Serve pancakes with butter, maple syrup, and/or jam.

Chicken Lots of Ways, and a Duck

Everyone's favorite feathered friend is present and accounted for: roasted, flattened, slow-cooked, flashed in the pan, and broiled till crisp.

Rack-roasted chicken with gravy potatoes	163
30-minute spatchcock chicken and vegetables	164
Chicken cutlets with spicy coconut dressing	167
Pan-fried chicken thighs with Italian salsa	168
Rosemary chicken ragu with pressure cooker polenta	170
Spice-drawer chicken wings	175
My way duck confit	176

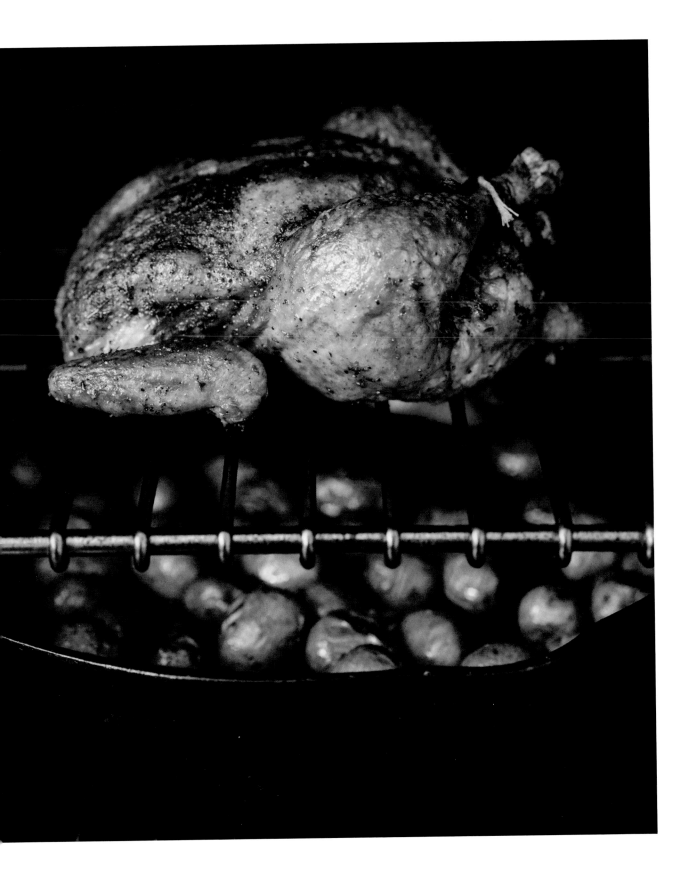

Rack-roasted chicken with gravy potatoes

Despite what you've read or choose to believe, there are *lots* of good ways to roast a chicken. This easy, slow-roasted method affords the bird a couple of hours to arrive at a shreddable tenderness reminiscent of rotisserie chicken. The chicken's perch on the oven rack lets heat circulate all around, while a side dish of potatoes, positioned just below, makes magic with all the chicken juices.

3 to 4 servings

From the Market
Chicken
Waxy potatoes

Spin It
Replace the potatoes with whole peeled shallots, trimmed leeks, scrubbed carrots, halved parsnips, 2-inch wedges of winter squash or scrubbed beets, halved firm apples (such as Pink Lady), or quartered cauliflower or Romanesco

At Home
Paprika
Oregano
Salt and pepper
Olive oil
Lemon

Spin It
Smoked paprika, Aleppo pepper, ground cumin, or crushed fennel seeds in place of either the paprika or the oregano

1 whole chicken (3½ to 4½ pounds)
2 teaspoons sweet paprika
1 teaspoon dried oregano
Kosher salt, freshly ground pepper
1½ pounds small waxy potatoes, such as Yukon Gold, scrubbed
1 tablespoon extra-virgin olive oil
1 lemon, cut into wedges

Season chicken inside and out and all around with paprika, oregano, and plenty of salt and pepper. Tie legs together, if desired. Place on a large plate or rimmed baking sheet and let sit to come to room temperature, about 1 hour. (Or refrigerate, uncovered, for up to 2 days.)

Position two racks in bottom third of oven and preheat to 325°F.

Place potatoes in a shallow ovenproof dish or rimmed baking sheet and season with salt and pepper. Add a splash of water to the dish and place on the lower of the two racks. Rub chicken with olive oil and place onto the rack directly above the potatoes. Roast until chicken is very brown and falling-apart tender and a thermometer inserted into thickest part of the breast registers somewhere around 205°F (yes, that's way above the usual 165°F target for chicken; it will be tender and on the verge of falling apart, but past peak juiciness), 2½ to 3 hours. Potatoes should

be very tender and sitting in a generous amount of lovely chicken juices.

Transfer chicken to a platter and let rest 20 to 30 minutes so that juices can redistribute and it's not too hot to carve.

While chicken rests, carefully pour off liquid from potatoes into a measuring glass. Use a wide shallow spoon to skim off some of the fat that rises to the surface (chill these drippings and use for another roasting project—they're essentially seasoned schmaltz). Taste chicken gravy and season with salt and pepper. Carve chicken and serve with potatoes, gravy, and lemon wedges for squeezing over.

30-minute spatchcock chicken and vegetables

Removing the chicken's backbone lets you open it like a book, flatten it, and cook it in half an hour at high heat. Ask whoever is at the meat counter to do this for you—you want it "spatchcocked" or "butterflied." To do it yourself, use a pair of kitchen shears to cut along either side of the backbone (Google it!). Almost any vegetable will roast in the same amount of time as long as it's cut into two-inch pieces; see Spin It for some ideas.

2 to 4 servings

From the Market
Chicken
Beets

Spin It
2-inch pieces of butter-
   nut squash, halved
   carrots, or small
   potatoes for all or
   some of the beets
Fennel or acorn squash
   wedges, cauliflower
   florets, or whole
   Brussels sprouts for
   all or some of the
   beets
Torn radicchio or
   escarole leaves, savoy
   or napa cabbage
   leaves, or kale leaves
   for all or some of the
   beets
Add a thinly sliced
   lemon to the
   vegetables

At Home
Fennel seeds
Crushed red pepper
Salt and pepper
Olive oil

Spin It
Aniseeds, cumin
   seeds, or coriander
   seeds can replace
   the fennel seeds

2 teaspoons fennel seeds
1 teaspoon crushed red pepper
1 whole chicken (3½ to 4½ pounds),
   backbone removed
Kosher salt, freshly ground pepper
8 to 10 medium beets, any color,
   greens trimmed
4 tablespoons extra-virgin olive
   oil, divided

Set oven racks in upper third and lowest position of oven, place a 10-inch cast-iron skillet on lower rack, and preheat oven to 500°F. (A preheated skillet jump-starts the browning process and dramatically reduces cooking time.)

Lightly crush fennel and crushed red pepper in a mortar and pestle or spice grinder. Season chicken on both sides with salt and black pepper, then with fennel–crushed red pepper mixture. Scrub and peel beets and cut into 2-inch wedges (quarters or sixths, depending on their size). Toss beets and 2 tablespoons oil on a rimmed baking sheet. Season with salt and pepper.

Carefully remove hot skillet from oven and place on the stovetop over high heat. Pour in remaining 2 tablespoons oil. Carefully lay chicken in skillet, skin side down. Use a spatula to press firmly down on chicken to make sure skin is in firm contact with pan. Cook until edges of skin are golden brown, about 2 minutes. Lay a sheet of foil over chicken, then place a second cast-iron pan, Dutch oven, or other heavy pot on top as a weight. This will help chicken maintain contact with the pan while it roasts, shortening the cooking time and helping the skin brown.

Return pan to lower rack and cook for 30 minutes. A thermometer inserted into thickest part of breast, avoiding bone, should register 150°F; temperature will continue to climb when chicken is resting. Roast beets on upper rack until tender when pierced with a cake tester, 25 to 30 minutes.

Turn chicken skin side up and let rest for 20 minutes. Serve with beets and any accumulated juices in skillet.

Chicken cutlets with spicy coconut dressing

Don't shake the can of coconut milk before opening it—you'll use the layer of cream on top in this sweet and spicy dressing, which is mellowed by the cooling iceberg lettuce and rich dark-meat chicken. Transfer the unused coconut milk to a clean jar and refrigerate it for making soup or a curry (it will hold for several days).

2 servings

From the Market
Red jalapeño
Chicken thighs
Iceberg lettuce
Cilantro

Spin It
Thin, boneless pork
    chops for the chicken
6 to 8 cups savoy
    cabbage leaves
    or romaine hearts
    instead of iceberg
2 English hothouse
    cucumbers or an
    8-inch piece daikon,
    thinly sliced, instead
    of iceberg
Mint and/or basil
    instead of cilantro

At Home
Garlic
Ginger
Unsweetened coconut
    milk
Lime
Salt
Unsweetened shredded
    coconut
Olive oil

Spin It
Thinly sliced shallot
    instead of garlic
Unseasoned rice
    vinegar for lime juice
Fish sauce in addition
    to salt for the
    dressing

½ red jalapeño, Fresno, or serrano
    chile, finely grated
1 garlic clove, finely grated
1-inch piece fresh ginger, peeled
    and finely grated
4 tablespoons coconut cream
    from 1 small can unsweetened
    full-fat coconut milk
¼ cup fresh lime juice, plus
    wedges for serving
Kosher salt
2 tablespoons unsweetened
    shredded coconut
4 boneless, skinless chicken
    thighs, patted dry
2 tablespoons extra-virgin olive oil
½ head iceberg lettuce, leaves
    torn into palm-size pieces
Handful of cilantro leaves and
    tender stems, torn

In a large bowl, combine chile, garlic, ginger, coconut cream, and lime juice. Season with salt and stir to combine. Stir in coconut and taste dressing: It should be fairly tangy, spicy, and salty to balance the mild iceberg. Dressing may seize and seem very thick, but it will loosen up when tossed with the salad.

Working with one thigh at a time, place chicken between two sheets of plastic wrap and use a meat mallet or rolling pin to pound out to ½-inch thickness. This will shorten cooking time and creates more surface area for crisping. Season cutlets on both sides with salt.

Place a 10- or 12-inch skillet, preferably cast-iron, over medium-high heat. Add oil and when it shimmers, place cutlets carefully into pan and cook, undisturbed, until well browned on underside and almost completely cooked through, about 5 minutes. Turn chicken and cook for about 1 minute on second side. Transfer cutlets to a platter or two dinner plates.

Add iceberg and cilantro to bowl with dressing and toss to coat. Taste the lettuce and add more salt and/or lime juice if needed. Serve cutlets and salad with lime wedges for squeezing over.

Pan-fried chicken thighs with Italian salsa

Chicken thighs are the best—juicy, flavorful, and crowned with a generous swath of skin that gets fantastically crisp. There's just one problem: Grocers sell thighs either bone-in and skin-on or boneless and skinless. The ideal situation, in my book, is boneless and skin-on, and until the rest of the world catches on, that means one extra step at home. For quick cooking plus crisp skin? Worth it.

2 to 4 servings

From the Market
Cherry tomatoes
Basil
Chicken thighs
Green beans

Spin It
1½ roughly chopped tomatoes for the cherry tomatoes
Replace half the basil with parsley
1 small fennel bulb, thinly sliced, for the green beans

At Home
Garlic
Olive oil
Salt and pepper
All-purpose flour
Red wine vinegar

Spin It
Half a small red onion, thinly sliced, for the garlic
Lemon juice or white wine vinegar for the red wine vinegar

---

12 ounces cherry tomatoes, halved, divided
4 garlic cloves, 1 finely grated, 3 thinly sliced
2 tablespoons extra-virgin olive oil, divided
Handful of basil leaves
Kosher salt, freshly ground pepper
4 bone-in, skin-on chicken thighs, patted dry
¼ cup all-purpose flour, for dusting
8 ounces thin green beans, trimmed, halved crosswise
1 tablespoon red wine vinegar

Toss half of the cherry tomatoes with the grated garlic, 1 tablespoon olive oil, and basil. Season with salt and pepper. Let salsa sit so tomatoes release some juices and flavors can marry.

Meanwhile, debone the chicken thighs: Working with one thigh at a time, place a chicken on a cutting board, skin side down. Press your finger against the flesh to locate the thigh bone that runs from one end to the other. Using a sharp paring knife, make short swift cuts along the length of the bone on one side to separate the flesh. Rotate chicken 180° and repeat on other side of bone. Wiggle the tip of your knife underneath the bone, angle blade upward, and cut bone out completely. Place thigh on a large plate and repeat with remaining thighs.

Place flour on a dinner plate. Season chicken on both sides with salt and pepper, then dredge very lightly in flour, patting excess off until only a sheer coating remains. Heat a large skillet, preferably not cast-iron, over medium-high heat. Pour in remaining 1 tablespoon olive oil, then lay thighs into pan, skin side down.

Cook chicken, undisturbed, until skin is deep golden brown and flesh is cooked about halfway through, 6 to 8 minutes. Turn chicken and cook on second side until chicken is cooked through, about 4 minutes more. Transfer thighs to a platter.

Return pan to medium-high heat and cook green beans, shaking pan occasionally, until charred in spots, 4 to 5 minutes. Season with salt and pepper. Add sliced garlic and reserved (plain) tomatoes to pan. Season again with salt and pepper and cook until tomatoes begin to soften and garlic is translucent, 1 to 2 minutes. Remove pan from heat and stir in vinegar, scraping up any browned bits in pan.

Serve chicken thighs with beans and tomatoes, with fresh tomato salsa spooned over.

Rosemary chicken ragu with pressure cooker polenta

The great thing about making a ragu from dark-meat chicken instead of red meat is that it takes a third of the time to cook, but it starts the same way—by browning the protein slowly and deliberately, and using that time to prep the vegetables that sweeten and deepen the sauce. In case that is all sounding too old-world for you, I've busted out my trusty pressure cooker to make a pot of polenta in less time than it takes to brown the chicken skin. Balance!

4 servings

From the Market
Pancetta
Chicken thighs
Fennel
Rosemary

Spin It
Chicken quarters or boneless, skinless thighs would also work
For a pork ragu, use 2-inch pieces of boneless shoulder
Celery, carrots, or chard stems can replace the fennel
Other hearty herbs like thyme or oregano can sub for rosemary, or just add them

At Home
Salt and pepper
Garlic
Onion
Crushed red pepper
Olive oil
White wine
Canned tomatoes
Polenta

Spin It
Red wine would be just as good as white; use whatever you're planning to drink
Use 2 cups chopped fresh tomatoes in place of canned
In place of polenta, serve over rice, white beans, or mashed potatoes

P.C. and Me

It was love at first chickpea for me and pressure cooking, and I'm still awed by the stupid-simple science at work: When you combine heat and moisture in a sealed pot, the combination of pressure and steam drastically reduces cook times without sacrificing flavor or quality. I use my pressure cooker at least once a week to make things like dried beans, chicken stock, polenta, sweet potatoes, whole grains, pork ribs, and soup. I am partial to my manual, stovetop model because it reaches pressure quickly and fits on the shelf with my other pots and pans. Electric multicookers (such as the Instant Pot) run on autopilot, which is nothing short of a luxury.

4 ounces pancetta or slab bacon,
  cut into 1-inch pieces
2 pounds bone-in, skin-on chicken
  thighs, patted dry
Kosher salt, freshly ground pepper
6 garlic cloves, smashed
1 small onion, finely chopped
1 small fennel bulb, tops trimmed,
  finely chopped
Crushed red pepper
1 sprig rosemary
Extra-virgin olive oil, as needed
½ cup white wine
1 (14-ounce) can whole peeled
  tomatoes
2 cups polenta (not quick-
  cooking)

Place pancetta in a large Dutch oven or other heavy pot with a lid over medium heat. Cook until fat renders and pancetta is golden brown and starting to crisp, about 8 minutes. Transfer to a small plate with a slotted spoon; pour drippings into a heat-proof bowl.

Spoon 1 tablespoon drippings back into pot and return to medium heat (save remaining drippings—liquid gold!). Season chicken with salt and pepper and cook, skin side down, until very well browned, about 10 minutes. Don't rush this step or crank the heat; cooking over medium heat will give the skin time to render while gradually taking on color. This is a great time to chop the vegetables and lay your hands on remaining ingredients.

Turn chicken and cook until second side is golden brown, about 6 minutes. Transfer to a plate (the thighs won't be cooked through yet). Add garlic, onion, and fennel to renderings in pot. Season with salt and cook, stirring with a wooden spoon and scraping up browned bits, until vegetables start to release some liquid, about 3 minutes. Add a big pinch of crushed red pepper and the rosemary and cook until onion is translucent everywhere and starting to brown on edges, 5 to 6 minutes. Use the edge of a wooden spoon to smash garlic into smaller pieces. If at any time pan looks dry, drizzle in some more of reserved drippings or olive oil to get things moving again.

Add wine, increase heat to medium-high, and simmer until almost completely evaporated, about 4 minutes. Add tomatoes and their liquid, then fill tomato can halfway with water to rinse, and pour that liquid into pan, too. Add half the reserved pancetta and stir to combine (set remaining pancetta aside for serving). Nestle thighs into sauce, skin side up, so that flesh is submerged but skin is exposed. Drizzle in any accumulated juices from plate. Bring liquid to a very gentle simmer, then cover pot and cook until chicken is totally tender and sauce is thickened, about 1 hour 30 minutes.

Meanwhile, combine polenta and 9 cups water in a pressure cooker, season generously with salt, and whisk well to combine. Bring to a simmer over medium-high heat (if using an electric pressure cooker, use the sauté function), whisking frequently. Seal lid and cook at high pressure for 9 minutes. Release pressure naturally, then remove lid and whisk polenta until creamy and homogenous. Taste and season with salt and pepper. (If you don't have a pressure cooker, use a large pot. Bring water to a simmer, season with salt, then slowly stream polenta into water, whisking constantly. Simmer, whisking very frequently, until polenta is tender, 35 to 40 minutes.)

Remove chicken from sauce and coarsely shred meat (discard skin and bones). Return chicken to sauce. Serve ragu over polenta, with reserved pancetta on top.

Chicken Lots of Ways, and a Duck

Spice-drawer chicken wings

Chicken wings have the ideal fat-to-flesh ratio, which is a roundabout way of saying that I love chicken skin. I came up with the dry spice mix on the fly one night (no pun intended, yuk yuk) after going "shopping" in my spice drawer, and it was good enough to make again. And again. The gingery cucumbers on page 99 are a good choice for a side dish.

4 to 6 servings

From the Market
Chicken wings
Mint and/or basil

Spin It
Chicken drumsticks
 for the wings
Omit the herbs, or
 use fennel fronds,
 cilantro, chives,
 or scallion greens
 instead

At Home
Salt
Oregano
Granulated garlic
Smoked paprika
Sugar
MSG
Grapeseed oil
Lime

Spin It
The truly essential
 spices are the paprika,
 the sugar, and the
 granulated garlic.
 If you don't have one
 of the others, don't
 sweat it.

1 tablespoon kosher salt
1 teaspoon dried oregano
1 teaspoon granulated garlic
1 teaspoon smoked paprika
1 teaspoon sugar
½ teaspoon MSG, plus more for
 serving
4 pounds chicken wings
2 tablespoons grapeseed oil
1 cup small fresh mint and/or
 basil leaves
2 limes, cut into wedges

In a small bowl, combine salt, oregano, granulated garlic, smoked paprika, sugar, and MSG. Pat chicken wings dry and arrange on a rimmed baking sheet lined with foil. Season on both sides with spice mix. Let wings sit 30 minutes at room temperature, or transfer to a zip-top bag and refrigerate for up to 24 hours.

Place racks in center and top positions of oven and preheat to 375°F. Drizzle wings with oil and toss to coat. Bake on center rack until wings are cooked through and skin is golden brown, about 30 minutes, turning with tongs halfway through. This initial cooking time renders some of the fat from the wings, which in turn allows the skin to crisp in next step.

Remove baking sheet from oven. Heat broiler. Broil wings on upper rack until skin is deeply browned and starting to char at edges, 5 to 7 minutes, turning wings every 2 to 3 minutes (because there is sugar in the rub, and because every broiler is different, this could happen very quickly; watch closely).

Transfer the wings to a platter and top with herbs. Serve with lime wedges for squeezing over.

My way duck confit

There was a day, many years ago, when I felt like preparing duck confit, but I didn't want to make a special trip and shell out big bucks for the quart (or more) of duck fat that most recipes call for. "Won't the duck make enough of its own fat?" I thought lazily. I decided to try it. I added a splash of water to the pot with the duck legs to help the fat render early on, covered the pot, and took it very low and slow. Whaddya know—it worked. Traditionalists will say this is a hack recipe, and that's fine. It's a shortcut, but it works just as well as the original. Another word for that is . . . improvement.

6 servings

From the Market
Duck legs
Thyme

Spin It
Rosemary or lemon
thyme for the thyme

At Home
Salt and pepper
Ginger
Chile de árbol
Garlic
Olive oil

Spin It
Other aromatics such as
lemongrass, juniper
berries, or bay leaf
can be added instead
of or in addition to
the ginger
If you don't like spice,
omit the chile
Whole shallots can
replace the garlic

Good Fat

Every time you brown a batch of chicken thighs, sear a steak, cook bacon or pancetta, or pan-roast a pork chop, you will be left with pan drippings. Unless the skillet is scorched, you want that fat. Pour it through a fine-mesh sieve into a clean jar, stick a label on it, and pop it in the fridge or freezer. Use the fat to make a confit, to roast or sauté vegetables, for refried beans or fried rice, or to cook down a sofrito for a soup or braise. As long as you use a clean utensil every time you dip into the jar, the renderings will keep for months in the refrigerator, and up to a year in the freezer.

6 Pekin duck legs, thawed if
  frozen
5 tablespoons kosher salt
1 tablespoon freshly ground
  pepper
1 bunch thyme
2-inch piece fresh ginger, peeled,
  cut into ¼-inch rounds
3 dried chiles de árbol
1 head garlic, halved crosswise
Olive oil, as needed

A day or two before making the confit, place duck legs in a small rimmed baking sheet or 9 × 13-inch dish and prick skin all over with a paring knife or carving fork, being careful not to puncture flesh. Make sure to get into the crook where the thigh and drumstick meet, and where there's usually a pocket of fat. Season with salt and pepper. Rub all over with a few sprigs of thyme (reserve remaining thyme). Cover duck and chill overnight (or for up to 2 days). The recipe will work if you skip this step, but the duck won't be as flavorful. Facts.

Preheat oven to 250°F.

Choose a heavy lidded pot that's just big enough to hold the duck legs in one snug layer—a little overlap is okay, since they will shrink as they cook, and a tight fit is preferable to having too much room. Pour in ¼ cup water. Add ginger, scatter remaining thyme sprigs over, then add chiles, crumbling them a bit with your fingertips as you go. Brush excess salt and thyme from duck and arrange legs in pot, skin side down. Tuck garlic halves around duck.

Cover pot and bake for 1 hour. Remove pot from oven and check progress: The duck will render a lot of fat during this time and should be about halfway submerged. Use tongs to nestle legs into fat and rearrange if needed so that they're all happily tucked in. Cover pot, return to oven, and bake 1 hour more.

Remove pot from oven to check duck. Turn legs skin side up; they should be just covered in their own fat by now. If not, add olive oil to cover (or use any drippings that you've been saving for an occasion like this one). Cover pot and cook until duck legs wiggle freely at the joint, flesh is shreddable, and skin is golden brown, 2 hours more (4 hours total time).

Carefully transfer duck to a clean vessel, preferably one that is glass or ceramic so that the confit doesn't pick up any off-flavors. Strain cooking liquid over (the legs should be submerged; add olive oil to cover if needed). Place garlic halves and ginger into liquid. Use immediately or let cool in liquid, then cover and refrigerate for up to 3 weeks (fat will solidify, sealing the legs).

To serve, heat a heavy skillet over medium heat until surface is warm. Tease duck legs out of fat, scraping excess back into container (if they've been chilled), and cook, skin side down, until skin is browned and very crisp, about 6 minutes. Carefully turn legs over and cook until warmed through, about 2 minutes more.

Serve legs with a knife and fork, perhaps on a bed of saucy lentils. Or, shred meat and serve with salad greens and a mustardy dressing. Make a duck taco! You could toss the meat into a tomato-based pasta sauce. Make duck hash! Make duck fried rice! Or wait until you're alone and eat duck with your fingers.

Fishes and Other Sea Creatures

Give me your fin fish, your mollusks, and your cephalopods. Once on land, we can get down to the best ways to enjoy them.

Seared scallops with brown butter, hazelnuts, and chives	183
Crispy-skinned black sea bass with salt-and-butter radishes	184
Pan-roasted salmon with cauli-tartar sauce and chive vinaigrette	187
Paprika plancha shrimp with basil mayo	188
Buttery pan clams with ginger and scallions	191
Grilled squid salad with cucumbers, herbs, and smoky chickpeas	192

Seared scallops with brown butter, hazelnuts, and chives

Dry scallops are fresh, unadulterated, highest-quality scallops, and they are the only ones to use in this dish. If they're not labeled dry, that means they've been treated with a liquid preservative that will ruin any hope you have of getting a good crusty sear on them (and that stuff doesn't taste so nice, either). Ask before you buy.

4 servings

From the Market
Large dry sea scallops
Chives

Spin It
Small bay scallops
   (cook time will be
   1 to 2 minutes total)
Parsley in place of
   chives

At Home
Salt and pepper
Grapeseed oil
Butter
Hazelnuts
Lemon

Spin It
Olive oil or canola oil for
   grapeseed
Almonds or pine nuts
   for the hazelnuts
Omit nuts altogether
Unseasoned rice
   vinegar or fresh
   grapefruit juice for
   lemon juice

1 pound large dry sea scallops
Kosher salt, freshly ground pepper
2 teaspoons grapeseed oil
3 tablespoons unsalted butter
¼ cup raw hazelnuts, roughly
   chopped
¼ cup fresh lemon juice, plus
   more if needed
Handful of chives, thinly sliced

Use your fingers to pull off the side muscle from the scallops and brush away any stray bits of shell or grit. Pat scallops dry with paper towels, then arrange on a large plate and season both sides with salt and pepper.

Heat a medium skillet, preferably stainless steel, over medium-high heat for a couple of minutes. When a drop of water dances on the surface of the skillet, add oil, which should immediately thin out and shimmer. Carefully place scallops into pan, flat side down, and cook, undisturbed, until you can see that they're dark brown on the edge that's in contact with the pan, about 4 minutes. Using a pair of tongs, a thin spatula, or a metal spoon, turn scallops onto second side and cook until just barely cooked through,

about 1 minute more. Transfer to a serving plate.

Pour off any residual oil from skillet and place over medium heat. Add butter and nuts to pan and cook, stirring often, until butter foams and then darkens, and nuts are lightly toasted, about 3 minutes. Add lemon juice and cook, scraping up any browned bits with a wooden spoon, until sauce is slightly thickened, about 30 seconds. If sauce reduces too much or looks thick and greasy, stir in a couple tablespoons of water to loosen and reemulsify. Add chives and taste sauce; adjust with more lemon juice or salt as needed.

Spoon pan sauce and nuts over scallops to serve.

Crispy-skinned black sea bass with salt-and-butter radishes

The flavor of cooked radishes can be a bit gassy (they're in the cabbage family, after all). Raw ones can be sharp and pungent. What's a girl to do?! This recipe splits the difference, sautéing them enough to mellow their bite, but maintaining enough crunch to contrast with a delicate fish fillet. Starting the fillets in a barely warm skillet keeps the skin from curling up, which helps it brown and crisp, a trick I learned from my esteemed colleague Chris Morocco.

4 servings

From the Market
Radishes
Black sea bass
Scallions
Chives

Spin It
2 watermelon radishes for small red ones
1 small piece daikon or kohlrabi for radishes
Skin-on striped bass, red snapper, branzino, or trout for black sea bass
Mint, basil, cilantro, or dill for chives

At Home
Grapeseed oil
Butter
Salt and pepper
Flaky sea salt
Lime

Spin It
Ghee in place of oil and butter
Lemon or a wedge of grapefruit for lime

---

1 bunch small radishes, any type or color, tops removed, scrubbed
1 teaspoon grapeseed oil
2 tablespoons unsalted butter, divided
4 skin-on black sea bass fillets (6 to 8 ounces each)
Kosher salt, freshly ground pepper
1 bunch scallions (white and pale-green parts only), thinly sliced crosswise
Small handful of chives, thinly sliced
Flaky sea salt, for serving
1 lime, cut into wedges

Thinly slice radishes and soak them in a medium bowl of ice water for 5 minutes, which will firm them up and reduce their spiciness. Drain and blot dry with a clean kitchen towel or paper towels.

Put oil and 1 tablespoon butter in a large nonstick skillet and place over medium heat. Pat fish dry on both sides with paper towels, season with salt and pepper, and place, skin side down, into pan. Gently press on fillets with a flexible spatula to encourage skin to make contact with skillet's surface. Cook, gently pressing down occasionally, until skin is very brown and crisp and flesh is opaque except for a thin strip down middle of flesh side, 6 to 8 minutes. Carefully turn fillets and cook on flesh side until just cooked through, about 1 minute longer. Transfer fillets to four plates or a serving platter.

Wipe out skillet and place over medium-high heat. Add remaining 1 tablespoon butter. When it begins to foam, add radishes and scallions, season with salt and pepper, and cook, tossing, until scallions are just wilted and radishes soften enough to be bendable but still have some crunch, about 2 minutes. Spoon radishes and pan sauce over and around fish and top with chives and a pinch of flaky sea salt. Serve with limes for squeezing over.

Pan-roasted salmon with cauli-tartar sauce and chive vinaigrette

When I crave salmon, I want the flesh rare in the middle, the skin to be sleek as glass, and the belly part of the fillet rich, fatty, and juicy. For me, only pan-roasting will do. It's worth paying a little bit more for well-sourced salmon. If the price per pound is too good to be true, the fish is probably not too good.

4 servings

From the Market
Salmon fillets
Fresno chile
Cauliflower
Dill and/or basil
Chives

Spin It
Steelhead trout, arctic char, or red snapper for salmon
Any other medium-spicy fresh chile can replace Fresno
Green cabbage for cauliflower
Tarragon, chervil, or fennel fronds to replace some or all herbs

At Home
Grapefruit
Sugar
Salt and pepper
Mayonnaise
Unseasoned rice vinegar
Capers
Olive oil

Spin It
A combination of orange and lemon zest and juice for grapefruit
Cider vinegar for rice vinegar
Chopped cornichons or brined green olives for capers

1½ pounds skin-on salmon fillets, patted dry
1 Fresno chile, finely chopped, seeds removed if desired
1 tablespoon finely grated grapefruit zest
2 tablespoons fresh grapefruit juice, divided
Pinch of sugar
Kosher salt, freshly ground pepper
½ head (about 1 pound) cauliflower, halved through the crown
3 tablespoons mayonnaise
4 tablespoons unseasoned rice vinegar, divided
1 tablespoon capers, drained and chopped
½ cup packed chopped tender fresh herbs, such as dill and/or basil
3 tablespoons extra-virgin olive oil, divided
1 bunch chives, thinly sliced

Preheat oven to 450°F. Place salmon skin side up on a plate and let sit while oven preheats. In a small bowl, stir together chile, grapefruit zest, 1 tablespoon grapefruit juice, and a pinch of sugar. Season generously with salt. Set chile-grapefruit mixture aside.

Meanwhile, place cauliflower halves cut side down and thinly slice, working from an outside edge toward the stem. You'll end up with pieces of all sizes, which is great. Place in a medium bowl and toss with a 4-finger pinch of salt. Let sit for 10 minutes, tossing a couple of times, then add mayonnaise, 2 tablespoons rice vinegar, capers, and chopped tender herbs. Set aside.

Preheat an 8- or 10-inch ovenproof skillet over medium-high heat for 2 minutes. Pat salmon skin dry again and season with salt and pepper. Add 1 tablespoon oil to skillet, then gently lay salmon skin side down in pan. Cook, undisturbed, until the skin is golden brown around edge, about 2 minutes. Transfer to oven, still skin side down, and cook until skin is very crisp and fish is medium-rare in thickest part, 7 to 10 minutes. Remove skillet from oven and gently turn fish onto flesh side. Let sit in skillet for 30 seconds, then transfer to a plate. Let salmon rest, skin side up, for 5 minutes.

In a bowl, stir together chives and remaining 2 tablespoons oil. Add remaining 1 tablespoon grapefruit juice and 2 tablespoons rice vinegar, season with salt, and stir chive vinaigrette gently to combine.

Add reserved chile-grapefruit mixture to cauliflower mixture and toss cauli-tartar sauce to combine. Serve salmon with cauli-tartar sauce, with chive vinaigrette spooned over.

Paprika plancha shrimp with basil mayo

My advice is to make this when you can get your hands on really good head-on shrimp, and I would insist on eating them with your fingers, picking up the heads to suck out the sauces, and drinking cold beer out of the bottle with your messy, schmeary hands.

4 servings

From the Market
Basil
Head-on shrimp

Spin It
Use chives, parsley, or tarragon instead of basil
Use large shell-on shrimp without heads and cook for half the time

At Home
Egg
Garlic
Lemon
Salt
Grapeseed oil
Butter
Pimentón de la Vera
Sherry vinegar

Spin It
Use 1 cup store-bought mayonnaise and skip the mayo making
Canola or peanut oil instead of grapeseed
Use ground cumin or ordinary smoked paprika in place of pimentón

1 large egg yolk
1 small garlic clove, finely grated
1 lemon, halved
Kosher salt
1 cup plus 2 tablespoons grapeseed oil, divided
½ cup finely chopped fresh basil
2 pounds large head-on, shell-on shrimp (about 16)
3 tablespoons unsalted butter, at room temperature
1 teaspoon hot pimentón de la Vera (picante)
2 tablespoons sherry vinegar

In a medium bowl, whisk together egg yolk, garlic, the juice of ½ lemon, and a pinch of salt. Whisking constantly, very slowly stream in 1 cup oil, doling it out drop by drop until mixture starts to look glossy, light, and slightly thickened (these are all signs that the emulsion has been achieved). Continue whisking, adding the oil a bit faster, until mayonnaise is thick and all the oil has been incorporated. Taste and season with salt and/or more lemon. Fold in the basil; set mayo aside.

Preheat a large cast-iron skillet over medium-high heat for 3 minutes. Add remaining 2 tablespoons oil, then immediately add shrimp to skillet, season with salt, and cook, undisturbed, until shells are a ruddy brownish-red color on underside, 2 to 3 minutes. Using tongs, turn shrimp and cook until shells are darkened, you can see juices bubbling along the crease where body and head come together, and flesh is opaque, 3 to 4 minutes more. Transfer shrimp to a platter.

Remove skillet from heat and let cool for 2 minutes (the sauce will scorch if you skip this cool-out period). Add butter and pimentón to skillet and place over medium heat. Cook for 1 minute, stirring up any browned bits in pan. Add vinegar and ¼ cup water, swirl to combine, bring to a bare simmer, then pour pan sauce over shrimp. Squeeze remaining ½ lemon over and serve with basil mayo for dipping.

Buttery pan clams with ginger and scallions

Sometimes I grill clams directly on the grates, but it drives me nuts when they unhinge and tip over and sacrifice their precious liquor to the coals. Cooking them in a skillet set on the grill is a great compromise—and a smart way to corral all that goodness (if you wish, do this inside on the stove). Eat this with bread for dipping in the ginger-scallion pan sauce.

4 to 6 servings

From the Market
Serrano chile
Scallions
Clams
Crusty bread

At Home
Olive oil
Ginger
Garlic
Butter

Spin It
Use a couple of shallots, a leek, or a handful of ramps in place of the scallions, and omit garnishing the finished dish with them raw
6 pounds mussels instead of clams

Spin It
A few slices of bacon, cut into pieces, a spoonful of black bean paste, or some miso can replace the ginger and/or garlic

2 tablespoons olive oil, plus more for drizzling
2-inch piece fresh ginger, peeled and crushed
3 garlic cloves, smashed
1 small serrano chile, thinly sliced
2 bunches scallions (white and pale-green parts only), thinly sliced, divided
4 dozen littleneck or Manila clams, scrubbed
Thick slices of rustic country bread, for dipping
4 tablespoons (2 ounces) unsalted butter

Prepare a grill for medium-high direct heat. (If you don't have a grill, do everything as written on your stovetop.)

Place a large cast-iron or heavy stainless steel skillet on grill grates and add oil. When oil is hot, add ginger, garlic, chile, and half of scallions and stir until vegetables are sizzling, about 1 minute. Add clams and ½ cup water (or white wine, if you have a bottle open), toss to coat, and cover skillet with a lid, baking sheet, or large piece of foil. Cook, checking and stirring every few minutes, until the clams begin to open, 5 to 10 minutes. Transfer cooked clams to a large shallow bowl or platter with a slotted spoon as they open, but be quick about it. If you end up with a couple stubborn clams that refuse to open,

discard them. They might be filled with sand, or they might be conscientious objectors. Either way, don't eat them. Keep pan sauce warm, off to the side.

Drizzle bread generously with oil on both sides. Place over direct heat and grill until golden brown and delicious looking on both sides, 2 to 3 minutes (or toast in a toaster and then drizzle with oil). Set aside.

Add butter to pan sauce and slide skillet back over direct heat. As soon as butter is foaming, about 1 minute, return clams and any accumulated liquid to sauce, shower with remaining scallions, and toss to coat. Serve clams with bread and a large empty bowl for discarding the shells.

Grilled squid salad with cucumbers, herbs, and smoky chickpeas

Don't be squeamish about squid: It is incredibly affordable, very accessible, mild flavored, and sustainable. The best ways to cook it are hot and fast or low and slow. This is an example of the first way—keep your paws off of it until grill marks appear on the first side, at which point it will be almost completely cooked through.

6 servings

From the Market
Squid
Persian cucumbers
Thai basil
Mint

Spin It
2 English hothouse cucumbers instead of Persian
Use cilantro leaves and stems in place of or in combination with the herbs
Lemon or lime juice for sherry vinegar

At Home
Salt and pepper
Garlic
Canned chickpeas
Olive oil
Pimentón de la Vera
Sherry vinegar

Spin It
Day-old bread, torn into ½-inch pieces, can replace the chickpeas
Hot Hungarian paprika can replace the pimentón
Cider vinegar or unseasoned rice vinegar for the sherry vinegar

2 pounds squid, bodies and tentacles separated
5 Persian (mini) cucumbers, roughly chopped
Kosher salt, freshly ground pepper
1 garlic clove, finely grated
1 (15.5-ounce) can chickpeas, rinsed, drained, and patted dry
3 tablespoons extra-virgin olive oil, divided, plus more for drizzling
½ teaspoon hot pimentón de la Vera (picante)
Leaves from ½ bunch Thai basil
Leaves from ½ bunch mint
2 tablespoons sherry vinegar, plus more to taste

Halve squid bodies lengthwise so that the bodies can open up like a book (it's okay if they don't lie completely flat). Rinse bodies and tentacles, pat dry, and arrange in a single layer on a rimmed baking sheet. Refrigerate squid. Place cucumbers in a sieve or colander, season with salt, and add garlic, tossing to coat. Let cucumbers sit until they release some liquid and absorb seasoning, 10 to 30 minutes.

Meanwhile, prepare a grill for medium-high direct heat. In a medium bowl, toss together chickpeas, 2 tablespoons oil, pimentón, and salt to taste. Place a small skillet on grill grates. When pan is hot, add chickpeas and cook, stirring occasionally, until they're toasty and crisp on the outside, 6 to 10 minutes. Transfer chickpeas to a serving bowl.

In a large bowl, toss squid with remaining 1 tablespoon oil and season with salt and pepper. Clean and lightly oil grill grates. Grill squid, undisturbed, until undersides are charred and squid releases easily from grates, 3 to 5 minutes. Turn onto second side and cook 30 seconds. Transfer squid to bowl with chickpeas. Add cucumbers, Thai basil, mint, and sherry vinegar. Drizzle salad with oil and toss gently to combine. Taste and adjust seasoning with more salt and vinegar, if desired.

Main Meats

High steaks, tender chops, and big roasts—this is what you'd call an omnivore's delight.

Pork steaks with snap pea and scallion salsa   197

Glazed and charred St. Louis pork ribs   198

Butter-basted rib eye with crunchy fennel salad   200

Slow-roast beef ribs with melted peppers and horseradish   204

Grilled short ribs with serrano-cilantro marinade   208

Pork and brisket bollito misto   210

Herbaceous grilled lamb chops   214

Slow-roasted lamb shoulder and beans with magic green sauce   216

Seared lamb patty with marinated Halloumi and herbs   221

Pork steaks with snap pea and scallion salsa

I was reporting a story with chef and restaurateur Rachel Yang the first time I had grilled pork shoulder, which I thought of as a strict braising cut. I was pretty dubious as she cut the shoulder into fat slabs, then marinated them with *gochujang* before putting a crisp char on them, but they were spicy and juicy and pleasantly chewy. Life changing! This recipe reminds me of how lucky I am to work in an industry where people are constantly teaching me new tricks.

6 servings

From the Market
Boneless pork shoulder
Scallions
Sake
Gochujang
Sugar snap peas

Spin It
Thick-cut pork rib chops or bone-in beef strip steaks instead of pork shoulder
¼ cup sriracha for gochujang

At Home
Salt
Garlic
Ginger
Miso
Mirin
Canola oil
Sherry vinegar
Toasted sesame oil

Spin It
Unseasoned rice vinegar and a dash of sugar for mirin

For the pork
3 pounds boneless pork shoulder
Kosher salt
4 bunches scallions, white and green parts separated
3 garlic cloves, smashed
2-inch piece fresh ginger, peeled and chopped
½ cup sake or water
½ cup gochujang
¼ cup miso
½ cup mirin
¼ cup plus 2 tablespoons canola oil, divided

For the salsa
Kosher salt
1 pound sugar snap peas, trimmed, thinly sliced
4-inch piece fresh ginger, peeled, coarsely grated
2 tablespoons sherry vinegar
4 teaspoons toasted sesame oil

Prepare the pork
Cut pork into ¾-inch-thick slices, place in a zip-top bag, and season lightly on both sides with salt. Roughly chop scallion greens (set whites aside for salsa). In a food processor, combine scallion greens, garlic, ginger, sake, gochujang, miso, mirin, and ¼ cup oil and process until smooth, about 1 minute. Pour marinade over pork and turn to coat. Seal bag and refrigerate for at least 2 hours or up to a day.

Make the salsa
Bring a medium pot of water to a boil and season generously with salt. Fill a medium bowl with ice water. Cook sugar snap peas until they turn bright green and no longer taste raw, about 1 minute. Drain and transfer to ice bath to cool. Drain and pat dry. Dry bowl and put peas into it.

Thinly slice scallion whites and add to snap peas along with ginger, vinegar, and sesame oil. Toss to combine, taste, and season with salt. Cover and chill.

Remove pork from marinade, scraping off excess. Heat a medium cast-iron skillet over medium-high heat. Add oil, then cook pork until deeply browned on underside, about 5 minutes (because of the sugar in the marinade, there may be charred spots, but don't let the surface get too dark). Turn and cook until well browned on second side and pork is medium-rare, about 5 minutes more. (Yes—you can eat pork that isn't gray, dry, and tough inside!)

Transfer pork to a platter and let rest 10 to 15 minutes. Cut against the grain into ½-inch-thick slices and serve with snap pea salsa for spooning over.

Glazed and charred St. Louis pork ribs

I like St. Louis ribs because they've got plenty of meat on top of the rib bone, and plenty of fat to prevent them from drying out. By teaming up your pressure cooker (or multicooker) and your broiler, you can have shreddy, falling-apart ribs on a weeknight. True story! If you don't have a pressure cooker or a multicooker (yet), wrap the ribs in a double layer of foil and bake on a rimmed baking sheet in a 300°F oven until very tender, about three hours. The subsequent steps are the same.

4 servings

From the Market
St. Louis pork ribs

Spin It
Use baby back ribs instead; pressure cook for 10 minutes or bake for 2 hours before broiling

At Home
Salt
Fish sauce
Cider vinegar
Brown sugar
Butter
Cayenne
Mustard seeds

Spin It
Use white distilled vinegar instead of cider vinegar
Use maple syrup instead of brown sugar
Ground mustard can replace mustard seeds

2 racks St. Louis pork ribs (about 5 pounds)
3 tablespoons kosher salt, divided
3 tablespoons fish sauce
3 tablespoons cider vinegar
3 tablespoons dark brown sugar
6 tablespoons (3 ounces) unsalted butter, melted
1½ teaspoons cayenne pepper
1½ teaspoons mustard seeds

Cut each rack of ribs in half between two center-most bones and season all over with 2 tablespoons salt.

Place a steamer insert in a pressure cooker and add 1 inch of water. Add ribs to pot, seal lid, and cook at high pressure for 12 minutes. Release pressure naturally. Transfer ribs to two foil-lined rimmed baking sheets. (At this stage ribs can be cooled, then covered and refrigerated for up to 2 days before proceeding, if you wish.)

Heat broiler.

In a small bowl, whisk together fish sauce, cider vinegar, brown sugar, melted butter, cayenne, mustard seeds, and remaining 1 tablespoon salt until sugar and salt dissolve. Brush or spoon half of mixture over both sides of ribs. Turn ribs meaty side up and broil until glaze is golden brown, about 4 minutes. Brush with remaining glaze and broil until ribs are dark golden and crisp, about 4 minutes more.

Let cool 5 minutes, then cut into smaller pieces to serve.

Butter-basted rib eye with crunchy fennel salad

What do these classics have in common: Duck confit and frisée. Breaded veal cutlet and tomato-arugula salad. Barbecue and pickles. Chicago-style hot dogs and this sassy little steak and salad dinner. Rich marbled meats are extra-delicious when served with cool, crunchy, acidic vegetables. It's a fact, and the combo never gets old.

3 to 4 servings

From the Market
Beef rib eye
Rosemary
Fennel

Spin It
This method works on any thick cut of steak or double-cut pork rib chops; cook pork to 130°F
Thyme can replace rosemary
Celery, radish, red cabbage, kohlrabi, or any other sturdy vegetable you like can replace the fennel

At Home
Salt and pepper
Olive oil
Butter
Garlic
Anchovy fillets
White wine vinegar
Aleppo pepper
Flaky sea salt

Spin It
A few drops of fish sauce instead of anchovies
Any mild chile or a few slices of fresh hot pepper instead of Aleppo
Sherry vinegar, red wine vinegar, or lemon juice for white wine vinegar

1 bone-in rib-eye steak, 2 inches thick (about 2 pounds)
Kosher salt, freshly ground pepper
⅓ cup extra-virgin olive oil, plus more for drizzling
3 tablespoons unsalted butter
4 garlic cloves, 3 smashed, 1 finely grated
2 or 3 sprigs rosemary
3 oil-packed anchovy fillets, finely chopped
2 tablespoons white wine vinegar
2 fennel bulbs
Aleppo pepper, flaky sea salt, and olive oil, for serving

If you think of it ahead of time, season the steak on all sides with salt and pepper and refrigerate, uncovered, for a few hours or up to 2 days. If not, no biggie. Season now and carry on.

Heat an 8- or 10-inch cast-iron skillet over medium-high heat for 2 minutes. Add enough oil to evenly coat pan with no bald spots and add steak. Cook, turning every 2 to 3 minutes, until a dark crust has formed on both sides and steak is very rare; a thermometer inserted dead center should register 115°F, 12 to 15 minutes. Turning the steak frequently will let you develop a gorgeous crust on the surface without creating thick strips of well-cooked steak, which is what can happen when you sear it very hard on one side and then the other. Plus, it will cook more evenly and in less time because the interior is being warmed gradually from both sides.

Reduce heat to medium and add butter, 3 smashed garlic cloves, and rosemary. Tilt the skillet toward you and scoot the steak to the far end of the pan so that the garlic and rosemary slide down into the foaming butter pooling at the front edge. Holding the skillet's handle with your non-dominant hand, use your other hand to spoon the butter up and over the steak repeatedly for 1 to 2 minutes, or until internal temperature hits 120°F for medium-rare. Transfer steak to a platter and let rest 15 minutes for juices to redistribute; temperature will climb a few degrees from carry-over cooking.

While steak rests, in a medium bowl, whisk together grated garlic clove, anchovies, and vinegar and season with a big pinch of salt. Whisk in ⅓ cup olive oil, then taste and season with salt and pepper. The dressing should veer on the punchy, acidic side.

Trim off dried-out woody ends of fennel stalks. Remove tough outer layer from fennel, then halve each bulb lengthwise through core. Cut a little V in root end to remove thickest part of core. Place each half cut side down and slice crosswise into ¼-inch-wide pieces, working from the tender tops all the way down to the stem end, and including the inner part of the core and fronds, which will give the salad a range of textures. Add fennel to bowl with dressing and toss to coat.

Cut steak away from bone and then slice against the grain into ½-inch-thick pieces. Top with fennel salad, some Aleppo pepper and flaky salt, and a drizzle of olive oil. Serve the bone, too, of course.

Slow-roast beef ribs with melted peppers and horseradish

I knew that short ribs were great when braised, but I had no idea that they could be slow-roasted to submission with hardly any liquid at all, until I saw chef Travis Lett (of Gjusta and Gjelina in Venice, California) do exactly that. Roasting eliminates the searing, deglazing, and sauce-building steps that can make braising a project, and gives you a chance to experience the flavor of the ribs without a lot of other ingredients elbowing to the front. Since then, I have short-ribbed in the summer and the winter, proudly instructing butchers to cut the ribs into long lengths for me, and never once have I had a less than stupendous result.

6 generous servings

From the Market
Beef short ribs
Star anise
Red bell peppers
Hot red chiles
Horseradish

Spin It
Use country-style pork ribs for the short ribs; total cook time may be shorter
1 teaspoon fennel seeds or aniseed for star anise
Other sweet peppers, such as cubanelles or poblano, can be used
Omit chiles and add another bell pepper
2 teaspoons prepared horseradish instead of fresh horseradish

At Home
Salt
Smoked paprika
Granulated garlic
Crushed red pepper
Olive oil
Lemon
Sherry vinegar

Spin It
Use sumac, ground cumin, or ground cinnamon for paprika
Use ¾ teaspoon cayenne for crushed red pepper
Use red wine vinegar for sherry vinegar

8 pounds English-style beef short
ribs, cut into 6-inch lengths
(about 6 ribs)
3 tablespoons kosher salt, plus
more for seasoning
2 whole star anise
1 tablespoon smoked paprika
1 teaspoon granulated garlic
2 teaspoons crushed red pepper
4 red bell peppers
3 small fresh hot red chiles, such
as Fresno
Extra-virgin olive oil, for drizzling
2-inch piece fresh horseradish,
peeled
1 lemon
¼ cup sherry vinegar, plus more
if needed

The night before you want to eat this dish—or the morning of—season short ribs on all sides with 3 tablespoons kosher salt. Finely grind the star anise with a mortar and pestle or in a spice grinder. Transfer to a small bowl and add the paprika, granulated garlic, and crushed red pepper. Season ribs with spice mix, packing it on and using all of it. Chill, uncovered, at least 4 hours and up to 2 days.

Position two racks in middle and top positions in oven and preheat to 300°F. Place ribs on a large rimmed baking sheet or in a roasting pan and pour in ½ cup water. Cover with foil, slide onto middle rack, and roast for 90 minutes.

Meanwhile, cut the bell peppers into thirds or quarters; remove stem, seeds, and any thick ribs. Cut hot chiles in half and use a paring knife to tease out seeds if you'd prefer less spice. Toss both types of peppers on a small rimmed baking sheet or large skillet with enough olive oil to coat generously. Season with salt and arrange peppers skin side up.

Once ribs have been cooking for 90 minutes, slide peppers onto top rack. Remove foil from ribs. Roast until peppers are collapsed but not shriveled, and edges and skin are charred in several spots, 90 minutes more. Take peppers out and check ribs: They should be pull-apart tender and there will be quite a bit of rendered fat in pan. (If not yet tender, return to oven and cook 30 minutes more, then check again.) Transfer ribs to a platter and pour cooking liquid into a liquid measuring cup or medium bowl. Use a soup spoon or small ladle to skim off as much fat as possible.

Roughly grate horseradish and lemon zest onto roasted peppers. Add sherry vinegar and toss to combine. Taste and season with salt and more vinegar, if desired. The peppers should be nice and bright to balance the richness of the ribs.

Cut meat off bones and then slice against the grain into ½-inch pieces. Return to platter and spoon defatted cooking liquid over. Serve with peppers.

Grilled short ribs with serrano-cilantro marinade

My favorite thing to order at Korean barbecue restaurants is kalbi—thin-cut, flanken-style short ribs that are damn tasty with or without a marinade. They are well marbled, super beefy, satisfyingly chewy, quick cooking, and take to marinades in almost no time, which makes them winners at home, too.

4 to 6 servings

From the Market
Serrano chiles
Sweet onion
Cilantro
Lemongrass
Flanken-style short ribs

Spin It
Jalapeño or Fresno chiles instead of serrano
Red onion in place of sweet onion
Thai basil, Italian basil, chives, or perilla leaves instead of cilantro
Extra ginger instead of lemongrass
Use ½-inch-thick pork chops, or other thin steaks such as flank or skirt, instead of short ribs, and take a few minutes off the total cook time

At Home
Mirin
Ginger
Vegetable oil
Salt

Spin It
2 tablespoons maple syrup instead of mirin
Turmeric or garlic instead of ginger
Soy sauce instead of salt

2 serrano chiles
½ sweet onion, roughly chopped
Fistful of cilantro leaves and stems, roughly chopped
3 lemongrass stalks, tough outer layer removed, lower third coarsely grated
¼ cup mirin
2-inch piece fresh ginger, peeled and roughly chopped
1 tablespoon vegetable oil, plus more for the grill
1 tablespoon kosher salt, plus more for seasoning
4 pounds thin-cut flanken-style short ribs (¼ to ½ inch thick)

In a food processor or blender, combine serranos, onion, cilantro, lemongrass, mirin, ginger, 1 tablespoon vegetable oil, and 1 tablespoon salt. Process until vegetables are very finely chopped. Place short ribs in a glass baking dish or zip-top bag and season with salt. Pour marinade over and turn ribs to coat. Cover and let sit at room temperature for 30 minutes, or refrigerate for up to 8 hours.

Prepare a grill for medium-high direct heat. Clean and lightly oil grates.

Transfer short ribs onto grill without scraping off marinade. Grill ribs, turning every 2 to 3 minutes or any time there's a flare-up and spooning any marinade left in dish onto them, until ribs have formed a dark crust and are lightly charred, 6 to 9 minutes for medium, depending on thickness. (If you don't have a grill, cook ribs in a lightly greased cast-iron skillet over medium-high heat, and be prepared for your kitchen to get smoky.)

Let ribs rest 10 minutes before serving.

Pork and brisket bollito misto

I wanted to name this surprisingly sexy pot of simmered meats The All-Time Greatest One-Pot Meal for Entertaining, but that title is a little long. The reason I wanted to call it that is because it checks all of my entertaining goals: I can make the entire thing in my "inside clothes" a day or two before friends are coming over; it requires mostly inactive time, so it's a no-brainer even on the day-of; the side dish is built in; and it delivers large-format drama when it hits the table.

8 generous servings

From the Market
Pork shoulder
Brisket
New Mexico chiles
Guajillo chiles
Habanero chiles
Savoy cabbage
Carrots
Waxy potatoes
Mostarda

Spin It
Any not-too-fatty braising cut of meat works well, either alone or combined: beef or lamb shanks, osso buco, boneless leg of lamb, short ribs. Follow the weights called for here and heed the visual cues; timing will vary.

A mix of earthy and spicy dried chiles is the goal: try chile de árbol in place of habanero; or ancho instead of guajillo, etc.

Choose any seasonal vegetable for simmering except beets, which will turn everything pink, and artichokes, which will flavor the broth in an unappealing way.

Dijon or country-style mustard can replace the mostarda

At Home
Salt and pepper
Garlic
Bay leaves
Oregano
Cumin seeds
Flaky sea salt
Dijon mustard
Cornichons

Spin It
Fennel seeds, coriander seeds, or mustard seeds can replace the cumin

Use any type of mustard that you like

Any pickled vegetable you like can be used in place of cornichons

3 pounds boneless pork shoulder

2 pounds brisket, preferably point end

7 teaspoons kosher salt, divided, plus more for seasoning

5 garlic cloves

2 dried New Mexico chiles

2 guajillo chiles

2 dried habanero chiles

2 bay leaves

2 teaspoons dried oregano

2 teaspoons cumin seeds

2 pounds carrots, peeled, green tops trimmed to ½ inch

3 pounds small waxy potatoes, such as Yukon Gold, scrubbed

1 small head savoy cabbage, leaves separated

Freshly ground pepper

Flaky sea salt, mostarda, Dijon mustard, and cornichons, for serving

Season pork and brisket with 5 teaspoons kosher salt total, rubbing it into the grain of the meat. Wrap meats separately in plastic wrap and refrigerate for at least 8 hours and up to 2 days. (The longer the better.)

In a large Dutch oven, toss together garlic, all the dried chiles, bay leaves, oregano, cumin seeds, and remaining 2 teaspoons kosher salt. Fill pot halfway with cold water and add meats. They should be covered by about 1 inch of water; if not, top off. Bring to a boil over high heat, skimming any foam or gray bits that rise to the surface, 10 to 12 minutes. Reduce heat immediately to the merest, daintiest hint of a simmer, with small lazy bubbles breaking the surface every few seconds (if you have a digital thermometer, liquid should hover between 200° and 205°F). Maintain this heat level, skimming surface occasionally and adding more water as needed to keep meat submerged, until pork is tender enough to shred easily with the tines of a fork, about 3 hours. Transfer pork to a platter or rimmed baking sheet and cover loosely with plastic wrap.

The brisket, by nature, will take longer. Continue to simmer until strands of meat can be easily torn off using a pair of tongs, about 1 hour more. Transfer brisket to platter with pork. Pour broth through a fine-mesh sieve into a large bowl or liquid measuring cup (discard solids).

Rinse out pot, pour strained broth back in, and return pork and brisket to pot. Let meats cool in liquid, then use a spoon to skim fat from surface. (If you'd like, cover and refrigerate meats in their broth for up to 3 days. Lift off solidified layer of fat and reheat gently until broth is warm before continuing.)

Transfer pork and brisket to a large plate. Place pot with broth over medium-high heat and bring liquid to a simmer. Add carrots and simmer until completely tender when pierced with a cake tester, 8 to 10 minutes. Transfer to a large bowl or platter with a slotted spoon. Simmer potatoes in broth until completely tender, 12 to 14 minutes. Transfer to bowl with carrots. Finally, simmer cabbage until thickest leaves are tender, 6 to 8 minutes. Taste broth and season with salt and pepper. Return carrots, potatoes, pork, and brisket to broth. Cover and keep hot over medium-low heat.

To serve, remove meats from broth and use a long sharp knife to thinly slice against the grain. Transfer to a large serving platter and season with flaky sea salt. Arrange carrots, potatoes, and cabbage all around. Ladle some broth over everything to moisten and rewarm. Serve bollito with flaky salt, mostarda, mustard, cornichons, and remaining hot broth at the table so everyone can customize their plates as they wish.

Herbaceous grilled lamb chops

Lamb chops cut from the rib section aren't cheap, so whenever I make this it feels like a special occasion, even when it's a Saturday night in the summer with my family. Try to get small lamb chops that have not been Frenched, or trimmed of the layer of fat and deckle that sits on top of the bone. That's the best part— lamb fat is king! This is a great springtime dinner with the asparagus on page 111.

4 servings

From the Market
Lamb chops
Mixed fresh herbs

Spin It
Lamb shoulder chops are good, too—not as tender but less expensive

At Home
Salt and pepper
Coriander seeds
Olive oil
Red wine vinegar

Spin It
Fennel seeds, sumac, cumin seeds, or mustard seeds can replace coriander
Use lemon wedges instead of vinegar

16 lamb rib chops, untrimmed (about 3 pounds)
Kosher salt, freshly ground pepper
1 teaspoon coriander seeds, lightly crushed
2 cups mixed chopped fresh herbs, such as rosemary, basil, mint, chives, dill, and/or parsley
½ cup extra-virgin olive oil
Red wine vinegar, for serving

Season lamb chops with salt, pepper, and coriander seeds and transfer to a glass baking dish or a large zip-top bag. Add herbs and olive oil and smush everything around to coat. Let sit at room temperature for 1 hour, or cover and refrigerate for up to 2 days.

Prepare a grill for medium-high direct heat. Lift chops out of marinade, letting excess drip off. Season lightly with salt. Grill, turning every 2 minutes, until chops are charred, fat is starting to render, and a thermometer inserted into center of chops registers 125°F for medium-rare to medium, 6 to 8 minutes. Transfer to a platter and season with a few dashes of red wine vinegar. Let rest for 10 minutes. I highly recommend eating these with your hands.

Slow-roasted lamb shoulder and beans with magic green sauce

Despite a slightly hefty-looking ingredient list, this is a hands-off, minimal-effort meal, perfect for Sunday dinners when you're not sure if four people or nine people will be at the table. The worst thing that can happen is that there will be shreddy meat leftovers and you'll get to make tacos or sandwiches or fried rice during the week. The magic thing about the green sauce is that it works seamlessly with any combination of tender herbs, so you can tweak it to your preferences, or for the herbs you happen to have on hand.

8 servings

From the Market
Lamb shoulder roast
Szechuan peppercorns
Thyme
Tender herbs
Serrano chile

Spin It
A similarly sized beef brisket (point end) or bone-in pork shoulder for the lamb
Black peppercorns instead of Szechuan peppercorns
Any tender herbs in any combination will work in the green sauce

At Home
Salt and pepper
Cumin seeds
Fennel seeds
Chiles de árbol
Soy sauce
Yellow onion
Garlic
Bay leaves
Large dried white beans
Olive oil
Capers
Nutritional yeast
Lemon

Spin It
Two oil-packed anchovy fillets for the capers
As long as there's a total of 5 tablespoons, you can adjust the ratio of cumin and fennel seeds
1 yellow onion for the shallots
Parmigiano for nutritional yeast

For the lamb
1 bone-in lamb shoulder roast
(6 to 7 pounds)
6 teaspoons kosher salt
3 tablespoons cumin seeds
2 tablespoons Szechuan
peppercorns
2 tablespoons fennel seeds
2 dried chiles de árbol
¼ cup soy sauce

For the beans and the green sauce
4 shallots, halved
1 head garlic, halved crosswise,
plus 2 garlic cloves, divided
2 bay leaves
Handful of thyme sprigs
1 pound dried large white beans,
such as gigante, rinsed, soaked
overnight if possible (see note,
page 151)
Kosher salt, freshly ground pepper
4 cups loosely packed tender
fresh herbs, such as basil, dill,
and/or parsley
½ serrano chile
¼ cup extra-virgin olive oil, plus
more for drizzling
1 tablespoon capers, drained
1 tablespoon nutritional yeast
1 lemon, halved

Make the lamb
Season lamb on all sides with 6 tea-spoons kosher salt; use all of it. In a small dry skillet, combine cumin seeds, Szechuan peppercorns, fennel seeds, and chiles and toast over medium heat, stirring constantly, until spices are slightly darkened and very fragrant, about 2 minutes. Transfer to a spice grinder or mortar and pestle and let cool, then finely grind. Season lamb all over with spice mixture, packing it on. Wrap lamb in plastic wrap (or use the butcher paper it came in) and let sit at room temperature for 2 hours, or refrigerate for up to 2 days.

Preheat oven to 325°F.

Place lamb in a large Dutch oven and pour soy sauce and ¼ cup water around. Transfer to oven and cook, uncovered, until lamb is pull-apart tender, very well browned, and a ther-mometer inserted into thickest part of roast registers 190°F, about 4½ hours. Continue to cook for 30 minutes more, which affords lamb sustained time at this key internal temperature to help melt the collagen and layers of fat within the roast; there's no danger that it will dry out despite the long roasting time.

Make the beans and the green sauce
Meanwhile, in a large pot, combine onion, halved head of garlic, bay leaves, thyme, beans, 1 tablespoon salt, and a few cranks of black pepper. Add water to cover beans by 2 inches and bring to a boil over high heat. Reduce heat to a very bare simmer and skim any foam that rises to the top. Cook, stirring occasionally and topping off

with water as needed, until beans are completely creamy and tender, but still intact, 40 to 50 minutes. Use a slotted spoon to fish out onion, garlic, bay leaves, and thyme, then taste beans and broth and adjust seasoning with salt and pepper.

While beans cook, in a blender, com-bine herbs, remaining 2 cloves garlic, chile, oil, capers, nutritional yeast, and juice of ½ lemon; season gener-ously with salt. Blend on medium-high speed until herbs are chopped, about 20 seconds. Add 3 ice cubes, increase speed to high, and blend until sauce is lightened, smooth, and creamy (add water a splash at a time to get things moving, if needed). The ice keeps the herb sauce cool so that it doesn't turn brown; it will liquefy as the blades turn, which helps with the texture of the puree. Cover green sauce and refriger-ate until lamb is ready.

For a more formal presentation, serve lamb whole and slice it at table. Or, use two forks or your fingers to shred lamb, then return it to pot with cooking liquid and toss to coat.

Drizzle beans with olive oil and juice from remaining lemon half. Season with more black pepper, and spoon some green sauce on top. Serve extra green sauce alongside.

Slow-roasted lamb shoulder and beans with magic green sauce; Pomegranate-parsley tabbouleh (page 155)

Seared lamb patty with marinated Halloumi and herbs

Because ground lamb contains a generous percentage of fat, you can smash it into a hot skillet and let it develop a nice crust without worrying about it drying out. Can't say that about ground turkey! Good lamb is naturally earthy and a little grassy, and its flavor won't get buried despite this big pile of fresh herbs and salty marinated cheese. If you are sensitive to even a whiff of gaminess, seek out domestic, grain-finished lamb, which is sweeter and milder than the 100 percent pasture-raised imports from New Zealand and Australia.

6 servings

From the Market
Halloumi
Ground lamb
Tender herbs

Spin It
Mild feta, queso fresco, or ricotta salata in place of Halloumi
Ground beef (20% fat) instead of lamb
Sliced scallion greens and/or Swiss chard leaves instead of herbs

At Home
Olive oil
Fennel seeds
Mustard seeds
Pepitas
Aleppo pepper
Lemon
Salt and pepper
Flaky sea salt

Spin It
Anise seeds or cumin seeds in place of fennel seeds
¼ teaspoon crushed red pepper for Aleppo
Chopped almonds or pistachios instead of pepitas
Lime zest and juice for lemon

6 ounces Halloumi, torn into small pieces
4 tablespoons extra-virgin olive oil, divided, plus more for drizzling
1 teaspoon fennel seeds
1 teaspoon mustard seeds
2 tablespoons pepitas (pumpkin seeds)
½ teaspoon Aleppo pepper
2 teaspoons grated lemon zest
Kosher salt, freshly ground pepper
2 pounds ground lamb
2 cups packed mixed tender herbs, such as dill, cilantro, and/or mint
Flaky sea salt and lemon wedges, for serving

Place Halloumi in a small heatproof bowl. In a small saucepan, combine 3 tablespoons olive oil, fennel seeds, mustard seeds, and pepitas and place over medium-low heat. Cook, stirring occasionally, until oil is sizzling, pepitas are golden brown, and some of the mustard seeds start popping, 3 to 5 minutes. Stir in Aleppo pepper and immediately scrape seasoned oil over Halloumi before chile has a chance to burn. Stir to combine, add lemon zest, and season with salt. Let Halloumi marinate while you make the lamb.

Heat a large (10- to 12-inch) skillet, preferably cast-iron, over medium-high heat for 3 minutes. Pour in remaining 1 tablespoon oil, add lamb, and use a spatula or the back of a wooden spoon to smash down, spread out, and flatten meat onto pan's surface. You're making a big flat lamb patty at this point. Season surface evenly with salt and black pepper and cook, undisturbed, until underside is very browned and you can see fat and juices start to pool on surface, 6 to 8 minutes. Toss lamb, using a spoon to scrape it up and break lamb into smaller pieces. Cook 1 to 2 minutes more, just to lightly sear rare side.

Transfer lamb to a platter. Spoon marinated Halloumi over, along with infused oil, pepitas, and spices. Top with the fresh herbs and a drizzle of olive oil. Season with flaky salt. Serve with lemon wedges for squeezing over.

Sunday Soups and Brothy Beans

For the love of legumes! If you serve it in a bowl and you eat it with a spoon, this is where you'll find it.

Pasta e fagiole	224
Green-estrone	228
Fox-style chickpeas	233
Yogi's kitchari with sizzled spices	234
Fresh corn and corn broth with popcorn spices	237

Pasta e fagiole

The first time I made pasta e fagiole was when I was in college and had dumbly realized that it was the only way I would get to eat it. I still have the handwritten notes from the call I made to my mom, asking for her recipe. To this day I prepare it the way she described: with dried beans, a pork product, a long-cooked sofrito, a tangle of kale, and plenty of small pasta added at the end. This is a soup you start around lunchtime on Sunday and look forward to eating that night for dinner.

4 generous servings

From the Market
Carrots
Leek
Ham hock
Kale

Spin It
1 fennel bulb or
   2 celery stalks can
   supplement or
   replace the carrots
1 large yellow onion can
   replace the leek
4 ounces bacon ends,
   pancetta, or sausage
   meat in place of the
   ham hock
A sprig or two of thyme
   or rosemary can be
   added
A few chopped Swiss
   chard stems can be
   added to the sofrito
Escarole for the kale

At Home
Dried white beans
Salt and pepper
Garlic
Olive oil
Canned tomatoes
Parmigiano rind
Bay leaves
Ditalini

Spin It
Green or beluga lentils,
   chickpeas, baby lima
   beans, or gigante
   beans instead of
   white beans. Cook
   time will vary; start
   checking after
   30 minutes.
1 teaspoon ground
   fennel added to the
   sofrito
Canned crushed
   tomatoes, or an
   equivalent amount
   of pureed fresh
   tomatoes (3 cups)
4-finger pinch of fresh
   thyme leaves or
   chopped rosemary
   instead of bay leaves
Orzo, small shells,
   pipette, or any other
   small dried pasta can
   replace ditalini

8 ounces dried medium white beans, such as cannellini, soaked overnight if possible (see note, page 151)

Kosher salt

6 garlic cloves

4 carrots, scrubbed, roughly chopped

1 leek (white and pale-green parts only), halved, rinsed, and roughly chopped

⅓ cup extra-virgin olive oil, plus more for serving

Freshly ground pepper

1 smoked ham hock

1 (15-ounce) can whole peeled tomatoes

1 bunch kale, leaves stripped off stems

1 or 2 Parmigiano rinds (optional)

2 bay leaves

8 ounces small pasta, such as ditalini

Parmigiano, crusty bread, and crushed red pepper, for serving

If you haven't soaked the beans, do a power soak: Put beans in a large pot, cover with water by 1 inch, and bring to a boil over high heat. As soon as water comes to a boil, turn off heat, stir in a palmful of salt, cover pot, and let beans sit for 1 hour.

In a food processor, combine garlic, carrots, and leeks and pulse until vegetables are finely chopped.

In a soup pot or Dutch oven, heat ⅓ cup olive oil over medium and add chopped vegetables. Season generously with salt and pepper and cook, stirring often, until vegetables start to sweat out some of their liquid, 3 to 5 minutes. The goal at this stage is to slow-cook the sofrito until vegetables are very soft but do not take on any color. This gives the dish depth. Cover pot and cook over medium-low heat, stirring every 5 minutes or so, until sofrito is softened and juicy, about 15 minutes. Reduce heat if mixture starts to brown. Add ham hock and cook uncovered, stirring and scraping surface of pot every 5 minutes, until sofrito is starting to brown in places and has lost at least half its volume, about 10 minutes more.

Add beans and their soaking liquid, tomatoes, and kale and season again with salt and pepper. Bring to a boil, then add Parm rinds (if using) and bay leaves and reduce heat to a very gentle simmer. Cook soup with lid askew until beans are very tender, 1 to 3 hours, depending on the size and age of the beans. Add water (or stock, if you have it) as necessary to keep beans submerged by at least 1 inch.

In a pot of well-salted boiling water, add pasta and set a timer for 2 to 3 minutes less than package instructions (pasta should be very al dente). Drain pasta and add to soup, then taste and adjust seasoning. (Do not try to skip a step by cooking the pasta in the soup. The noodles will absorb all the available liquid and the liquid will be thick and gummy.) Serve with Parmigiano for grating over, bread for dunking, olive oil for drizzling, and crushed red pepper.

Green-estrone

This is spring's answer to minestrone—a place to put all of the very early season's green things that arrive when the weather is still a little chilly in the shade. I purposely combine longer-cooked vegetables with vibrant, barely cooked greens and herbs for a mix of sweet and bright notes.

10 servings

From the Market
Scallions
Ramps
Waxy potatoes
Bok choy
Haricots verts
Sugar snap peas
English peas
Chives

Spin It
Omit scallions or ramps and use 4 shallots or 1 red onion instead
Double up on chives in the herb oil
Any type of waxy potato will suffice, including fingerling, Yukon Gold, and butterball
Instead of bok choy, use one-quarter of a green cabbage, 1 bunch mature spinach, or 1 bunch kale
Any combination or type of snap beans and fresh peas can be used; the total weight should be between 1½ and 2 pounds
Instead of chives, use more scallion greens, more ramp leaves, or a tender herb
A spoonful of sour cream stirred into each portion is extremely delicious

At Home
Butter
Olive oil
Salt and pepper
Crushed red pepper
White wine
Parmigiano rind
Small pasta
Lemon
Flaky sea salt

Spin It
Instead of white wine, use water and a squeeze of lemon juice, or a tablespoon of dry vermouth
Break spaghetti or linguine into short lengths for the pasta
Instead of 2 quarts water, use a light-bodied homemade chicken stock or Parmigiano broth (that recipe is part of the Carbonara Stracciatella method on page 131)

1 bunch scallions, whites and
   greens separated
4 ounces ramps, trimmed
2 tablespoons unsalted butter
3 tablespoons plus 6 tablespoons
   extra-virgin olive oil, divided
Kosher salt, freshly ground pepper
12 ounces small waxy potatoes,
   such as Yukon Gold, peeled and
   cut into ½-inch-thick rounds
¼ teaspoon crushed red pepper
¼ cup white wine
2 bunches small bok choy
   (12 ounces total), sliced
   crosswise into ¼-inch pieces
4 ounces haricots verts or green
   beans, trimmed, cut into
   ¼-inch lengths
8 ounces sugar snap peas,
   trimmed, halved lengthwise
1 cup shelled English peas (from
   about 1 pound pods)
Parmigiano rind (optional)
8 ounces small pasta, such as
   ditalini or mini shells
Wide strip of lemon zest
1 bunch chives, very thinly sliced
Flaky sea salt, for serving

Slice scallion whites crosswise into thin rounds (set tops aside). Cut ramp bulbs in half where the pink-hued part of the stem meets the base of the leaves. Slice any large ramp bulbs in half lengthwise. Cut ramp greens crosswise into 1-inch pieces; set aside.

In a large pot, melt butter and 3 tablespoons oil over medium heat. Add scallion whites and ramp bulbs and season with salt and pepper. Cook, stirring frequently, until the vegetables are softened and blond (don't let them brown), about 5 minutes. Add potatoes and stir to coat. Cook until potatoes have lost their starchy, matte appearance and cut surfaces look shiny, 1 to 2 minutes. Add crushed red pepper and wine and cook until wine is reduced by about half, 3 minutes more.

Add bok choy, haricots verts, sugar snap peas, and English peas and stir to coat. Season with salt and pepper and cook until bok choy leaves wilt and peas and beans are bright green, about 5 minutes. Add Parmigiano rind, if using, pour 2 quarts water into pot, and bring to a simmer over high heat, about 6 minutes. Reduce to a gentle simmer and cook until potatoes are completely tender but not falling apart, 10 to 12 minutes.

(Adding all of the green vegetables at once will result in wonderfully silky, very tender, and well-cooked vegetables, which is achieved at the expense of a vibrantly colored soup. It's also less fussy. Letting the vegetables cook together longer gives the soup a chance to develop true depth of flavor, even though the liquid used is plain old water.)

Meanwhile, bring a pot of well-salted water to a boil. Add pasta and set a timer for 2 to 3 minutes less than package instructions (it should be very al dente). Drain pasta and transfer to soup. Add ramp greens and lemon zest. Cook for 2 to 3 minutes to let flavors meld; stir in some water if soup looks too tight.

Thinly slice reserved scallion greens and stir together with chives and 6 tablespoons olive oil in a small bowl. Serve soup with a pinch of flaky salt and herb oil spooned over.

Fox-style chickpeas

I spent two days with vegetable whisperer Jeremy Fox, the chef at Rustic Canyon Wine Bar in Santa Monica, California, on an assignment for *Bon Appétit*, and will be forever grateful for his advice on cooking beans: "If the broth tastes good," he told me, "the beans will taste good." Letting the beans sit in the flavorful stock they've helped to create infuses them with flavor to their very center. The other key to cooking beans is patience—lower the heat to maintain the barest possible simmer, which will help keep the skins intact as they slowly soften.

8 servings

From the Market
Carrots
Thyme

Spin It
Sage, rosemary, basil, oregano, or parsley for the thyme

At Home
Dried chickpeas
Yellow onion
Garlic
Salt and pepper
Olive oil
Crushed red pepper

Spin It
Any dried bean, such as cannellini, cranberry, gigante, pinto, or black, for the chickpeas
2 shallots for the onion
A whole dried chile for the crushed red pepper

---

1 pound dried chickpeas, soaked overnight if possible, drained (see note, page 151)
2 carrots, halved lengthwise
½ large yellow onion, unpeeled
5 garlic cloves, peeled
1 tablespoon kosher salt, plus more to taste
Freshly ground pepper, extra-virgin olive oil, and crushed red pepper, to taste
Handful of thyme sprigs

In a large stockpot, combine chickpeas, carrots, onion, garlic, and 1 tablespoon salt and cover with cold water by 3 inches. Bring to a boil over medium-high heat, then immediately reduce heat to medium-low. Set the lid askew, and let beans simmer very, very gently—adding water to the pot as needed to keep beans submerged—until they are completely tender but not mushy, about 1 hour 30 minutes. (This may go faster if the beans have been soaked, or could take longer, depending on the age of the beans.) Avoid the urge to stir the pot. Agitation will cause the skins to split and the broth will be cloudy;

occupy yourself with something else to do and let time do its thing.

Remove pot from heat and season bean liquid purposely and fearlessly with salt, black pepper, olive oil, and crushed red pepper. The broth should be tasty enough to sip on its own. Squeeze the thyme in your hand to release its aromatic oils, then submerge into the broth and let the beans cool.

To serve, use a slotted spoon to scoop out onion, carrots, and thyme. Return liquid to a simmer over medium. Taste and adjust seasoning one last time.

Yogi's kitchari with sizzled spices

I was doing an Ayurvedic cleanse called *panchakarma* many years ago the first time I ever heard of, or made, *kitchari*, and it is to this day one of my essential feel-good foods. Mung beans, common in Indian and Chinese medicine, are detoxifying; the mix of spices is both warming and calming; white rice is easy to digest; and well-cooked vegetables (sans alliums or nightshade) are grounding and nourishing. If you feel off, or are coming back from a cold, or have been overindulging and want to give your system a break, this is what you should eat.

8 servings

From the Market
Carrots
Turmeric
Mung beans

Spin It
Winter squash, potatoes, fennel, green beans, sweet potato, kale, or bok choy can replace or supplement the carrots

At Home
Ghee
Ginger
Salt and pepper
Mustard seeds
Fennel seeds
Coriander seeds
Cinnamon
Basmati rice
Lemon

Spin It
Refined virgin coconut oil or extra-virgin olive oil to replace ghee

⅓ cup plus 3 tablespoons ghee, divided
4 medium carrots, cut into ½-inch pieces
2-inch piece fresh ginger, peeled and finely chopped
Kosher salt, freshly ground pepper
2 teaspoons mustard seeds, divided
1½ teaspoons ground turmeric, divided
1 teaspoon fennel seeds
1 teaspoon coriander seeds
½ teaspoon ground cinnamon
2 cups mung beans, soaked overnight if possible (see note, page 151)
1 cup basmati rice, rinsed in a large bowl until the water runs clear
Lemon wedges, for serving

In a large pot, melt ⅓ cup ghee over medium heat. Add carrots and ginger, season with salt and pepper, and cook, stirring, until carrots start to release some liquid, 2 to 3 minutes. Add 1 teaspoon each mustard seeds and turmeric. Add fennel seeds, coriander, and cinnamon and cook, stirring often, until carrots have softened and start to take on some color, 5 to 6 minutes. Add mung beans and rice and stir to coat, season again with salt, then add 3 quarts water and bring to a boil over high heat. Reduce heat to a simmer and cook, stirring occasionally and adding more water as needed if soup starts to tighten up, until beans are completely tender and rice is starting to fall apart, 30 to

45 minutes, depending on whether mung beans were soaked. Thin with more water as desired—this can be porridge-like or soupy, depending on your preference.

Meanwhile, in a small skillet or saucepan over medium heat, melt remaining 3 tablespoons ghee. Add remaining 1 teaspoon mustard seeds and ½ teaspoon turmeric and cook, stirring, until mustard seeds begin to pop, 1 to 2 minutes. Remove from heat and season spiced ghee with salt.

Divide soup among bowls and spoon some sizzled spices and seasoned ghee over. Serve with lemon wedges for squeezing over.

235 Sunday Soups and Brothy Beans

Fresh corn and corn broth with popcorn spices

Popcorn is my spirit food. I eat a giant bowl at least once a week, and it always makes me feel better, especially when I'm tired, cranky, hungry, happy, bored, antsy, filled with rage, or thrilled and delighted. Over the years, I've perfected the nutritional yeast–driven spice mix that I shower liberally all over my popcorn. Though my personal popcorn habits may not be of any concern to you, you'll be happy to know that the seasoning is quite flattering on this mash-up of fresh corn, sweet corn broth, and crunchy fried corn nuts.

4 servings

From the Market
Corn
Corn nuts

Spin It
Crushed tortilla chips, Fritos, popcorn, or potato chips can replace the corn nuts

At Home
Salt and pepper
Nutritional yeast
Aleppo pepper
Coriander seeds
Butter

Spin It
Grated Parmigiano for nutritional yeast
A pinch of cayenne for Aleppo pepper
A dollop of sour cream instead of butter

½ teaspoon kosher salt, plus more for seasoning
2 tablespoons nutritional yeast
1½ teaspoons Aleppo pepper
6 ears corn
1 teaspoon coriander seeds
Freshly ground pepper
2 tablespoons unsalted butter
½ cup large corn nuts (Quicos brand), lightly crushed

In a small bowl, stir together ½ teaspoon salt, nutritional yeast, and Aleppo pepper. Set the spice mix aside.

Cut kernels from cobs; you should have about 4 cups. Transfer to a medium bowl.

Place corncobs in a wide saucepan or medium stockpot and add water just to cover. Lightly crush coriander seeds in a mortar and pestle and add to pot. Bring liquid to a boil over high heat, skimming any foam that rises to surface, about 2 minutes. Reduce heat to a hard simmer, season with salt and pepper, and cook until liquid has reduced by about half and tastes positively corny, about 15 minutes. Strain broth into a liquid measuring cup.

Rinse out pot and return broth to pot. Add corn kernels and bring to a simmer over medium heat. Cook until corn is tender, about 4 minutes. Stir in butter and season to taste with salt and pepper.

Use a slotted spoon to transfer corn to a serving bowl, mounding it up in the center. Pour broth around base of corn mountain. Top with spice mix and a turn or two of black pepper. Top with corn nuts and serve with a big spoon.

Basic Baker's Sweets

Assuming you already have butter, flour, salt, and sugar in the house, you'll be able to pull off all of these simple desserts with a handful of additional ingredients and an entry-level skill set.

10-minute pastry dough	241
Any-fruit galette	242
Fruit compote with labneh, maple syrup, and olive oil	244
Coffee crème caramel	246
Birthday-worthy Swedish pancakes	250
Mom's cornmeal cream shortcake-biscuits	255
Praline meringues	256
Cinnamon spice and honey is nice brittle	260
Chocolate and vanilla mousse	263

10-minute pastry dough

When I use a food processor to make dough, I inevitably go too far—the butter is reduced to tiny bits, and the dough ends up unevenly or over-hydrated. These are pitfalls that lead to dense, tough crusts. When I work quickly with my hands, though, I can clearly feel, see, and control what's happening. The butter is coaxed into long, flat, steam-producing sheets, which create flaky layers in the crust (for step-by-step instructions and photographs, see page 75). I know what works for me, and I hope this method works for you, too!

*Makes enough for 1 large galette,
a 9-, 10-, or 11-inch tart, or a single-crust pie*

At Home	Spin It
All-purpose flour	½ cup whole wheat flour can replace ½ cup all-purpose flour
Salt	
Sugar	
Butter	Salted butter in place of unsalted butter; omit kosher salt
	Ice-cold vodka in place of water

1¾ cups all-purpose flour (spooned and leveled), plus more for surface
1 teaspoon kosher salt
1 teaspoon sugar
8 ounces cold unsalted butter, cut into 10 or 12 pieces

Dump the flour onto a clean work surface, sprinkle salt and sugar over, and toss with your fingers to distribute. Toss butter into the dry ingredients until each piece is coated with flour, then use a rolling pin to roll the butter into the flour until the butter is flattened into long, thin pieces. This will take several passes to achieve. Pause after every few rolls and use a bench scraper to help gather the mixture back together, and to scrape the work surface and rolling pin clean if butter and flour stick to it, which they definitely will. Rub the pin with more flour if needed. Work quickly so that butter doesn't become too warm. When the butter pieces are flattened and flexible (not soft and mushy), you've arrived. If you go too far, the butter will soften and start to melt, and you'll struggle with the next step.

Drizzle ¼ cup ice water over and use the bench scraper and your hands to toss mixture until water is evenly distributed. Some pieces of butter may bend and break into smaller pieces as you toss, which is totally fine. Roll dough out to a long rectangle about 10 inches wide, with a short side closest to you. Dust dough and work surface with flour as needed to prevent sticking, and scrape pin clean often. Using the bench scraper to help you, fold top third of dough (which will look like a crumbly pile of flour clumps) over the middle, then lift up bottom third and fold it up and over (as though you were folding a letter into thirds, but instead of paper, you had to fold wet pulp). Rotate dough 90 degrees and repeat rolling and folding, gathering loose bits of dough clumps in with the main part of the dough as you go. Do not balk or abandon the project if the dough is in tatters for at least the first two fold-and-turns. By the third rolling and folding, the dough may be a little crumbly along the long sides, but it should start to look relatively smooth and elastic in the center. Squeeze a knob of dough in your hand to see if it holds together. If not, repeat rolling and folding one or two more times and check again.

Loosen dough from surface and gather it into a disk, then wrap in plastic wrap and press down to 1 inch thick.

Chill dough at least 30 minutes and up to 2 days before rolling out to desired shape. Dough can be frozen for up to 3 months.

Any-fruit galette

Here is a galette you can make year-round, with the same dough every time and virtually any fruit that's in season, that will always work. The key is to bake the galette until the pastry is deeply browned—not blond, not golden. Browned. That will give it a crisp bottom and the best flavor. And if you go a little too far, remember: It's not burned, it's *bien cuit*.

8 servings

From the Market
Fruit

Spin It
½ vanilla bean, seeds scraped into the fruit mixture
Freshly ground black pepper added to the fruit (especially good with berries)

At Home
All-purpose flour
Citrus
Salt
Cornstarch
Butter
Sugar in the raw
Heavy cream, ice cream, crème fraîche, or yogurt

Spin It
1 teaspoon ground ginger or garam masala in place of citrus zest
Unseasoned rice vinegar, apple cider vinegar, or excellent balsamic vinegar, in place of citrus juice

Dough Before You Go
Turn to page 75 to see detailed instructions on making the dough for this galette, and page 78 for various fruit options.

10-Minute Pastry Dough (page 75), chilled, or thawed if frozen

All-purpose flour, for surface

2 pounds pears, apples, stone fruit (such as peaches, plums, apricots, and/or cherries), berries, rhubarb, figs, bananas, or oranges

1 to 2 teaspoons grated orange, lemon, or lime zest, plus 1 tablespoon juice (optional)

Pinch of kosher salt

2 teaspoons cornstarch (optional; for some fruits)

2 tablespoons unsalted butter

Sugar in the raw or granulated sugar, for sprinkling (optional)

Whipped cream, vanilla ice cream, crème fraîche, or full-fat Greek yogurt, for serving, optional

Roll out dough on a lightly floured surface to a 12- to 14-inch round, and don't worry too much about slight cracks that appear around perimeter. Dust surface and rolling pin with flour as needed to prevent sticking, and rotate dough 90 degrees often to help prevent wider cracks (every other roll wouldn't be overkill). If dough sticks to surface, gently lift it up from one side and scatter flour underneath before continuing. It should be approximately ⅛-inch thick. Roll dough onto your pin and unfurl it onto a sheet of parchment paper or a silicone baking mat. Slide dough and paper onto a rimmed baking sheet and refrigerate while you prep the fruit. (If you want to work further ahead, wrap the baking sheet tightly with plastic wrap, and keep dough refrigerated for up to 2 days before continuing.)

Preheat oven to 400°F.

Prep the fruit: If using apples, pears, or stone fruit, peel (if desired) and cut into ¼-inch wedges or slices. If using cherries, pit and leave them whole. Hull berries and cut large ones in half. Trim rhubarb, cut into 5-inch-long pieces, and halve lengthwise if stalks are fat. Cut figs in half and trim stems. For bananas, cut on an angle into ¼-inch-thick slices. Peel oranges and cut into rounds.

Place fruit in a medium bowl. Add citrus zest and juice (if using) and pinch of salt; toss gently to distribute. If using berries or very juicy stone fruit, add cornstarch and toss gently to coat.

In a small saucepan or skillet, melt butter over medium heat and cook, swirling pan often, until butter foams, turns golden, and then browns, about 3 minutes. Set aside.

Remove dough from refrigerator and scrape fruit onto center, then gently coax it toward edges, leaving a 3- to 4-inch border uncovered. Using the paper to help if needed, lift edges of the dough up and over fruit, working in 2-inch sections around circumference and overlapping dough slightly. Most of the fruit should still be uncovered.

Using a pastry brush, gently brush dough with browned butter, then dab it onto exposed fruit. Sprinkle sugar on fruit and all over surface of dough, if you like. It will add a little sparkle and crunch to the finished galette, but it's 100 percent extra.

Transfer baking sheet to oven and bake until crust is deep golden brown and fruit juices are bubbling, about 50 minutes. If it leaks, it leaks. That's what the parchment is for.

Let galette cool on baking sheet until slightly warm, then use a spatula to transfer to a baking rack to come to room temperature. (If there are a lot of juicy escapees that have caramelized on the paper, make sure to transfer the galette before they harden, fusing the galette to the surface.)

Cut galette into wedges and serve with whipped cream, vanilla ice cream, crème fraîche, or Greek yogurt, if desired.

Fruit compote with labneh, maple syrup, and olive oil

This compote starts with a dry caramel that is suspended with vinegar, which keeps it from being too cloyingly sweet. It's a perfect thing to put together when there are too many fruits and berries in the house in danger of going uneaten. I love it with tangy, rich labneh, the Lebanese strained yogurt, but it wouldn't be terrible spooned over vanilla ice cream, either.

Makes 2 cups

From the Market
Berries and/or stone fruit
Labneh

Spin It
Any juicy, ripe fruit is fair game, but don't use bananas (they're too starchy)
Ice cream, ricotta, or cottage cheese, for the labneh

At Home
Sugar
Unseasoned rice vinegar
Olive oil
Maple syrup
Flaky sea salt

Spin It
Cider vinegar or Banyuls vinegar instead of rice vinegar
Honey or pomegranate molasses instead of maple syrup

½ cup sugar, plus more to taste
1 tablespoon unseasoned rice vinegar, plus more to taste
12 ounces mixed juicy fruit (such as sliced peaches, blackberries, and/or strawberries)
2 cups labneh or Greek yogurt
Extra-virgin olive oil and maple syrup, for drizzling
Flaky sea salt, for serving

In a small heavy saucepan, heat sugar over medium-high heat, stirring occasionally from edge toward center, until sugar starts to liquefy. Continue cooking, stirring to encourage even browning, until syrup turns into a medium amber caramel, about 4 minutes. Carefully add vinegar (mixture will bubble up violently and seize). Reduce heat to medium, add fruit, and cook, stirring gently, until caramel relaxes and fruit is coated. Lower heat to medium and simmer until compote is thickened, fruit starts to break down, and mixture is very shiny and saucy, 6 to 8 minutes. Transfer to a heatproof container and let cool. Taste and season with more sugar and/or vinegar, as desired. (Compote can be covered and chilled for up to 1 week.)

To serve, divide labneh among bowls and use a spoon to carve out a swoosh on the surface of each. Spoon some compote over, then drizzle with olive oil and maple syrup. Crush a pinch of flaky salt on top.

Coffee crème caramel

My mom made crème caramel a lot when I was little, and I have very strong memories of sitting at the kitchen table and scraping away at the hardened caramel in the bottom of the ramekin with a spoon to get as much of the bittersweet sugary glaze as possible. My inspiration for this flavor was Häagen-Dazs coffee ice cream mixed with burned caramel. Baking it in a water bath is key for achieving that barely set, dense, and luscious consistency.

8 servings

From the Market
Vanilla bean

Spin It
Use 2 teaspoons vanilla extract instead of the bean

At Home
Coffee beans
Milk
Sugar
Lemon
Eggs

Spin It
Instead of coffee beans, you can infuse the custard with black tea or a spice, such as cinnamon, star anise, cardamom pods, or fennel seeds

For the coffee custard
¼ cup coffee beans, roughly
   chopped
2½ cups whole milk
½ cup granulated sugar
Wide strip of lemon zest
1 vanilla bean, split lengthwise
6 large eggs

For the caramel
⅔ cup sugar
1 teaspoon fresh lemon juice

Make the coffee custard
In a small saucepan, combine coffee beans, milk, sugar, and lemon zest. Scrape in vanilla seeds; add pod. Bring mixture to a gentle simmer over medium heat. Immediately turn off heat, cover pan, and let steep for 30 minutes.

Preheat oven to 325°F. Place a 1½-quart loaf pan inside an 11 × 13-inch baking dish, roasting pan, or other ovenproof dish with sides that are at least as high as loaf pan. You can also use a 9-inch pie plate set inside of a roasting pan. This is the setup for the water bath.

Make the caramel
In a small saucepan, combine sugar, lemon juice, and ¼ cup water. Cook over medium-low heat, stirring, until sugar is completely dissolved, 4 to 5 minutes. Do not rush this step; if liquid boils before sugar is dissolved, syrup may crystallize and never darken, and you'll have to start over.

When sugar is dissolved and syrup has gone from cloudy to clear, stop stirring and increase heat to medium. Cook, swirling pan every few minutes and giving caramel your full attention, until syrup begins to darken and gradually goes from amber to deep mahogany. When you see wisps of smoke rising from dark golden-brown caramel, immediately pour into prepared loaf pan. Quickly tilt pan back and forth to coat surface and a bit of the way up the pan's sides with caramel. Return pan to larger dish.

Finish the custard
Bring a kettle of water to a boil for the water bath.

Break eggs into a medium bowl and whisk just to break them up a bit. Reheat coffee mixture until steaming and then, whisking constantly, add it to the eggs. Whisk until mixture is completely combined, then pour through a fine-mesh sieve into caramel-lined loaf pan. Pour hot water into larger baking dish to come halfway up sides of loaf pan and transfer to oven. Bake until custard is mostly set but jiggles a bit at very center when you jostle pan, 1 hour 25 minutes to 1 hour 30 minutes. Let cool in water bath for 30 minutes, then remove, cover pan with a sheet of plastic wrap, and refrigerate crème caramel until completely set, at least 4 hours and up to 2 days.

To unmold, run a thin-bladed knife around edge of custard, making sure tip of knife reaches all the way down to caramel layer. Invert a larger plate or platter over loaf pan, then quickly, confidently, and optimistically turn plate and pan over in one motion, holding them together securely as you invert so that things don't slip around. Slowly lift off loaf pan and custard should slide out. If not, tap gently against countertop until it releases.

Serve crème caramel in slices, with caramel spooned over each piece.

Birthday-worthy Swedish pancakes

My husband's family, the Musics, celebrate birthdays with a Swedish pancake feast, to be enjoyed by the person of honor, ideally in bed, with a full array of fillings, toppings, and embellishments for customizing each crepe-like pancake the second it comes out of the pan. The tradition lives on at our house, where we spread out at the dining table, bowls and spoons within easy reach.

Makes 8 to 10 pancakes

From the Market
Bananas
Berries

Spin It
Use any ripe, fresh
    fruit you like; cut
    into thin wedges
    or small pieces

At Home
All-purpose flour
Sugar
Salt
Milk
Eggs
Butter
Vegetable shortening
Bacon
Lemon and lime
Peanut butter
Jam
Maple syrup
Heavy cream
Powdered sugar
Sugar in the raw

Spin It
Use any/all of the
    toppings suggested,
    or come up with your
    own (honey, caramel
    sauce, Nutella,
    sour cream, toasted
    nuts, etc.)

1½ cups all-purpose flour
  (spooned and leveled)
5 teaspoons sugar
½ teaspoon kosher salt
2¼ cups whole milk, plus more if
  needed
6 large eggs
6 tablespoons (3 ounces) unsalted
  butter, melted, plus more,
  softened, for serving
Vegetable shortening or ghee, for
  greasing
Assorted toppings, such as
  cooked bacon, lemon and lime
  wedges, peanut butter, bananas
  and berries, jam, maple syrup,
  whipped cream, powdered
  sugar, and sugar in the raw

In a blender, combine flour, sugar, salt, milk, eggs, and 6 tablespoons melted butter. Puree until mixture is smooth and bubbles form on top, about 30 seconds. Let batter rest at least 15 minutes at room temperature for flour to hydrate, which makes for more tender pancakes (or refrigerate in an airtight container for up to 1 day). After resting, whisk batter to combine; it should be the consistency of heavy cream (thin with more milk, as needed).

Heat a 12-inch stainless steel skillet over medium heat. Lightly coat with shortening. Add ⅓ cup batter and immediately tilt skillet in all directions so that batter spreads evenly across skillet's surface and into a round. Cook until underside is golden brown, 2 to 3 minutes.

Loosen edge of pancake with a heat-proof spatula, then grasp the edge between your fingertips and flip onto second side. Cook 1 minute more. Slide out of skillet and serve immediately. Repeat with remaining batter. (Grease skillet as needed.)

There is no point in trying to keep these warm for any length of time. Every person should get to garnish their pancake upon receipt, with the toppings they like. If you're not sure where to start, the Musics suggest a dusting of powdered sugar, a drizzle of maple syrup, and some lemon juice squeezed over.

Mom's cornmeal cream shortcake-biscuits

I grew up thinking that my mom was a biscuit wizard. I rarely saw her making them, but there they were on any given weekend morning, all tender and steaming inside, with crisp golden-brown bottoms. Her recipe is based on Marion Cunningham's Buttermilk Biscuits from the *Fannie Farmer Baking Book,* and my recipe is based on Mom's. I turned them into shortcakes, but the plain biscuits are an excellent breakfast option anytime.

8 servings

From the Market
Berries or plums

Spin It
Use any berry or stone fruit

At Home
Cornmeal
All-purpose flour
Salt
Baking powder
Sugar
Baking soda
Butter
Buttermilk
Heavy cream

Spin It
Omit the cornmeal and increase the flour to compensate
Whip together Greek yogurt and sour cream instead of whipped cream

For the biscuits
8 tablespoons (4 ounces) chilled unsalted butter, cut into ½-inch pieces, plus more for greasing
¼ cup fine- or medium-grind cornmeal, plus more for sprinkling
1¾ cups all-purpose flour (spooned and leveled)
1 teaspoon kosher salt
2 teaspoons baking powder
1 teaspoon sugar
½ teaspoon baking soda
⅔ cup buttermilk

For the fruit
1 pound berries, halved if large, or plums, cut into ⅛-inch-thick wedges
2 teaspoons sugar, divided
1 cup heavy cream

Position a rack in center of oven and preheat to 425°F. Lightly grease an 8-inch cast-iron skillet or cake pan with butter and scatter a 4-finger pinch of cornmeal across surface.

Make the biscuits
In a medium bowl, combine ¼ cup cornmeal, flour, salt, baking powder, sugar, and baking soda and toss with a fork to combine. Add butter and use your fingers to pinch and smash the butter into the dry ingredients, working quickly but determinedly until the butter is basically indiscernible and mixture feels fluffy. (Coating the flour with the butter, rather than leaving little pieces of butter in the dough, prevents gluten from activating and results in a super-tender but not especially flaky biscuit.) Pour the buttermilk over and use a fork to toss and mix until liquid is well dispersed and dough is starting to clump together.

Turn out dough onto a work surface and knead a few times just to bring it together. Don't overmix. Use a soup spoon, ¼-cup measure, or 2-ounce ice cream scoop to divide dough into 8 equal portions. Roll lightly between your palms to smooth edges and place, spacing evenly apart, in prepared skillet.

Bake biscuits until golden brown and puffed, 18 to 20 minutes. Let cool in pan until warm to the touch.

Meanwhile, prepare the fruit
Toss berries with 1 teaspoon sugar and let sit for 10 minutes to allow juices to release. Using electric beaters or a stand mixer, whip cream in a large bowl with remaining 1 teaspoon sugar until medium peaks form (if you have a stand mixer, use the whisk attachment; for handheld mixers, use standard beaters or whisk attachment).

Split biscuits and spoon fruit and fruit juices onto bottom halves. Spoon whipped cream over, add a little more fruit, then set the top half on top.

Praline meringues

For these meringues, bittersweet, salted candied almonds are reduced to crumbs and then folded into airy egg whites. While the meringues bake, the praline softens and creates little pockets of caramel crunchies inside. Yes, you're going the extra mile to make something that literally melts in your mouth, but that's what makes these so extra. Also, there will be praline left over for spooning over ice cream or yogurt on another day—who can resist a twofer?!

Makes 18 meringues

At Home
Butter
Almonds
Granulated sugar
Flaky sea salt
Eggs
Powdered sugar
Kosher salt
Vanilla extract

Spin It
Whole raw hazelnuts can replace the almonds
Almond extract can replace the vanilla

Making Meringue

Egg whites are pretty amazing. When whipped, the elastic proteins in the egg stretch out and trap air bubbles, creating a stable foam. The addition of sugar and use of a double boiler helps make a stable meringue, one that will be chewy and crunchy instead of dry and brittle. When beating the eggs, stop at the point when there's lots of air in the mixture but the whites are still stretchy and elastic. The meringue should look shiny and buoyant and the peaks should stand straight up—that's stiff peaks. There's no harm in stopping the beaters to check your progress every minute or so, just lift the beaters out of the mixture gently so you don't smash all those nice bubbles you're in the process of creating. This way, you'll avoid the dreaded overwhipped stage, when the proteins are stretched past their limit and the whites become grainy and watery. If that happens, start over—at least eggs don't break the bank.

For the praline
**Softened unsalted butter, for
  greasing**
1 cup whole raw almonds
½ cup granulated sugar
1 teaspoon flaky sea salt

For the meringues
**Softened unsalted butter, for
  greasing**
3 large egg whites
1½ cups powdered sugar
½ teaspoon kosher salt
1 teaspoon vanilla extract

Make the praline
Very lightly grease a small baking sheet with butter and set near the stove. In a medium saucepan, combine almonds, granulated sugar, and 3 tablespoons water. Cook over medium heat, stirring with a heatproof spatula until sugar dissolves and syrup is bubbling, then continue to stir until syrup thickens, about 3 minutes. Continue to cook, stirring, until syrup seizes up and becomes crystallized and sandy, about 3 minutes more. There will be no liquid: The nuts will be coated with a light sugar crust and there will be more sandy bits in the bottom of the pan and stuck to the sides. Stir until the sugar liquefies again and turns amber, 2 to 3 minutes. Cook, stirring to coat nuts with caramel, until they are shiny and turn a deep glorious mahogany color. Scrape praline onto prepared baking sheet, spread out, and season lightly but evenly with flaky salt. Let cool completely, then transfer to a food processor and pulse until finely chopped. Measure out ¾ cup praline crumbs (save leftovers for another use).

Make the meringues
Position a rack in center of oven and preheat to 350°F. Very, *very* lightly grease a large baking sheet or line with a sheet of parchment paper.

In a large glass or stainless steel bowl, combine egg whites, powdered sugar, and salt. Place bowl over (not in) a pan of simmering water and whisk until mixture is heated to 120°F, about 2 minutes (if you don't have a digital thermometer, test with your fingertips; it should be hot but not scalding). Heating the egg whites thoroughly dissolves the sugar and makes for a very shiny, stiff, and stable meringue.

Remove the bowl from heat. Use an electric mixer to beat egg whites on high speed until stiff peaks form, about 5 minutes (if you have a stand mixer, use the standard-issue mixer bowl and the whisk attachment; for handheld mixers, use standard beaters or whisk attachment). To check readiness of the meringue, invert beaters and assess: Whites should be thick, elastic, and glossy and should stand straight up without curling over at the peak. (If they resemble softly beaten whipped cream and slide down the beaters, you need to whip them longer. If they look grainy, dry, lumpy, or sag when inverted, they are overwhipped and the meringues will be flat and chewy.) Add vanilla and beat until stiff peaks form again, about 1 minute longer.

Remove bowl from mixer and sprinkle reserved praline crumbs over, then fold gently once or twice to distribute crumbs—it's okay if there are pockets of praline here and there. Use two large spoons to scoop up dollops of meringue and scrape them onto prepared baking sheet. Sprinkle a little more praline crumbs over, if desired.

Place meringues in oven, prop door open an inch or two with a pair of metal tongs or a rolled up kitchen towel, and bake until meringues puff, crack on outer edge, and feel dry to the touch, 15 to 20 minutes. Do not brown. Let meringues cool on sheet.

Cinnamon spice and honey is nice brittle

I have loved brittle ever since I was an eight-year-old at sleepaway camp, because that's what I got in my care packages. This one has good snap but won't bust a molar, and is seasoned aggressively with spices and chile to appeal to a slightly more adult palate.

Makes 6 cups

From the Market
Star anise

Spin It
Use ¼ teaspoon crushed red pepper instead of Maras or Aleppo

At Home
Butter
Sugar
Honey
Cinnamon stick
Maras pepper
Salt and pepper
Baking soda
Salted roasted peanuts
Pepitas
Flaky sea salt

Spin It
Light corn syrup can replace the honey
½ teaspoon ground cinnamon or ground cardamom instead of the cinnamon stick
Any combination of nuts and seeds can be used

6 tablespoons (3 ounces) unsalted butter, plus more, softened, for greasing
2 cups sugar
⅓ cup mild-flavored honey
1 cinnamon stick
2 pieces star anise (optional)
½ teaspoon Maras or Aleppo pepper
½ teaspoon freshly ground pepper
1 teaspoon kosher salt
1 teaspoon baking soda
6 ounces salted roasted peanuts
6 ounces toasted pepitas, pistachios, and/or whole almonds
Flaky sea salt, for topping

Place two pieces of parchment paper on a work surface and lightly grease each with a thin coating of butter.

In a deep saucepan, combine sugar, ⅓ cup water, 6 tablespoons butter, and honey and bring to a simmer over medium heat, stirring frequently with a heatproof spatula to dissolve sugar, 3 to 4 minutes. Add cinnamon and star anise (if using). Fit pan with a candy thermometer and cook, swirling pan every few minutes, until temperature hits 300°F, 6 to 8 minutes. Immediately stir in Maras pepper, black pepper, kosher salt, and baking soda and stir until combined, about 30 seconds (the baking soda will cause the caramel to foam up and bubble excitedly). Add all nuts and seeds at once and stir swiftly and thoroughly until nuts are completely coated, smoothing out any big clumps to make sure each nut is surrounded by caramel, about 1 minute.

Carefully but quickly scrape brittle out onto one piece of prepared parchment (it's extremely hot, so don't burn yourself, but work efficiently so that you finish this step before the brittle starts to cool and harden). Top with second piece of prepared parchment, buttered side down, then cover with a clean kitchen towel (for insulation) and use the palms of your hands or a rolling pin to spread out the brittle and flatten it to the thickness of a peanut. Peel off top piece of parchment and season brittle liberally with flaky salt. Let cool completely, 20 to 30 minutes, then break into shaggy pieces. If brittle bends instead of breaking, it needs more time to cool.

Chocolate and vanilla mousse

Mousse should be airy but thick, light on the tongue but richly flavored, smooth but also a little chewy. I'm certain the recipe I grew up eating was from *Mastering the Art of French Cooking*, which says to heat the egg yolks with sugar, beating until the mixture is thick and voluminous, which is where that stretchy texture comes from. This is an easy recipe to double, and you can make it in one large baking dish rather than in individual cups if you prefer.

6 servings

From the Market
Chocolate
Heavy cream

Spin It
To make mint whipped cream, add a handful of fresh mint to the unbeaten cream and chill it overnight. Strain before beating.

At Home
Butter
Vanilla extract
Kosher salt
Eggs
Sugar
Flaky sea salt

Spin It
Omit the vanilla and use almond or coffee extract instead

8 ounces semisweet or bittersweet chocolate, finely chopped
4 tablespoons (2 ounces) unsalted butter
2½ teaspoons vanilla extract, divided
½ teaspoon kosher salt, plus more for seasoning
4 large eggs, separated
½ cup sugar, divided
1 cup heavy cream
Flaky sea salt

In a large heatproof bowl, combine chocolate and butter. Place bowl over (not in) a pan of simmering water. Cook, stirring occasionally, until chocolate is completely melted and mixture is smooth and shiny, about 5 minutes. Remove from heat and stir in 1 teaspoon vanilla and ½ teaspoon salt. Let chocolate mixture cool. Don't dump the hot water; you'll use it again.

In a medium heatproof bowl, whisk together egg yolks and ¼ cup sugar. Place over (not in) same pan of simmering water and cook, whisking constantly, until mixture is very thick, lightened in color, and fluffy, and sugar is dissolved (rub a little between your thumb and forefinger to check), 3 to 4 minutes. Remove from heat and whisk in 1 teaspoon vanilla and a pinch of kosher salt. Let cool until warm, whisking occasionally.

Using electric beaters or a stand mixer, whip egg whites in a large bowl on medium speed until liquidy, about 1 minute (if you have a stand mixer, use the whisk attachment; for hand-held mixers, use standard beaters or whisk attachment). Add a pinch of kosher salt, increase speed to medium-high, and whisk until foamy soft peaks form, about 4 minutes. Gradually stream in remaining ¼ cup sugar and beat until stiff, shiny, glossy peaks form, about 4 minutes more. If you lift out a beater and invert it, the whites should look elastic and bouncy, but will stand straight up with a point that only hints at curling over.

Gently but thoroughly fold chocolate and egg yolk mixtures together until no streaks remain. Fold in one-third of egg whites until combined, then add remaining egg whites and gently fold *just* until no white streaks are visible, making sure to scrape spatula along bottom of bowl where chocolate tends to collect.

Spoon mousse into six 4-ounce ramekins, small jars, coffee cups, or any other individual vessels you want to use (or, make a family-style serving in a 1½-quart-capacity shallow bowl, pie plate, or other serving dish). Cover with plastic wrap and refrigerate until mousse is firm, at least 4 hours and up to 2 days.

When ready to serve, in a large bowl, with an electric mixer, beat heavy cream and remaining ½ teaspoon vanilla on medium-high speed until medium peaks form. Spoon whipped cream over mousse, dividing evenly, and top each with a pinch of flaky salt.

Acknowledgments

It would be impossible to list all of the purveyors who make me look forward to shopping for food on a regular basis, but I can try: Amber Waves Farm, Balsam Farm Stand, Berried Treasures, Cornuco Farms, Fishkill Farms, Gosman's, Hot Bread Kitchen, Lani's Farm, Lucky Dog Farms, Marlow and Daughters, The Meat Hook, Migliorelli Farm, Mountain Sweet Berry Farm, Paisanos Butcher Shop, Rancho Gordo, Ronnybrook Dairy, S & SO Produce Farms, Silamar Farms, She Wolf Bakery, Stokes Farm, Stuart Seafood Market, Toigo Orchards, and Wilklow Farms. They sell me the ingredients that inspire me to go home and cook for the people I love, which is my favorite thing to do.

To the thousands of cooks and eaters who follow me on Instagram and listen to the *Bon Appétit* fopodcast and watch my YouTube videos and send me questions and compliments and pictures of how my recipes turn out for them at home: Knowing that you trust my advice gave me a reason to write this book. Thank you.

To Adam Rapoport, who has consistently encouraged me to fight for the things I am passionate about and who told me to write the way I talk, which is the single best edit note I've ever gotten.

To the unparalleled group of food editors I've been honored to work with at *Bon Appétit*: Andy Baraghani, Molly Baz, Yekaterina (Kat) Boytsova, Brad Leone, Rick Martinez, Gaby Mélian, Chris Morocco, Claire Saffitz, and Anna Stockwell. You are the best in the business, and your collaborative creative process is a constant reminder that culinary knowledge is meant to be shared.

To Liesel Davis, the best recipe editor on planet earth, whose precision guided me when I was struggling to find the right words for my recipe instructions. And to Jill Baughman, a model of patience and steadiness.

To Julia Kramer, one of the great humans. You are a loyal confidante, solid comrade, and beloved friend, and you inspire me to be a better person, mostly because I want you to keep liking me.

To Christine Muhlke, for breaking bread with me for years, for listening and having my back, for being a connector, especially for women, and for knowing me well enough to know I should talk to Katherine Cowles.

And to Kitty, who is not only a book agent, but my agent of change, and who zeroed in on the crux of this book before I could even articulate it. Partnering with you was one of the best decisions I've ever made.

Thank you to Doris Cooper for finding scallion graveyards relatable and laughing at my dorky jokes, and most important for making a home for me at Clarkson Potter. Start to finish, I have felt completely tucked under your wing. You're good, you.

Potter's Erica Gelbard makes me feel like a burger that is about to get dressed with special sauce. Your enthusiasm is infectious—I'll do whatever you say.

To my beloved friends who encouraged and supported me and didn't get mad when they didn't hear from me for weeks and months on end: Leslie Robarge and Jon Feldman, Colu Henry, Vanessa Holden and Simon Andrews, Pat and Anne Keane, Chandra Kelemen, Delia and Pond Kelemen, Harry Lee, Jenn McCormick Panawek, Ruthie Vexler and Stu Zickerman, and Mary Wigmore.

And to my West Coast fam: Henrietta, Leilani, Roz, Sam, and Harvey Music, for rooting for me.

To Stephen Kelemen, the most expressive, passionate, inventive, intuitive, welcoming, hilarious, stylish home cook and baker in all the land. Being fed by you is the best.

To Bill Loscher and his family for trusting our family with the house on Fort Lane. I never slept or ate as well as I did during the summers we spent under that little roof. The recipes on pages 103, 118, and 147 belong to Billsville.

To Grace Robinson-Leo and Robert Matthews, the brilliant designers at Decade, for turning my awkwardly expressed ideas into a tangible, beautiful thing that looks and feels exactly the way I hoped, even though I could never have described it. Your design sensibility, amazing sense of style, and willingness to take risks motivated me throughout this process. The support and guidance of Melanie Glass made every step run smoothly.

To the incredible Andrea Gentl and Martin Hyers: Watching you at work made me realize what it means to be an expert. Thank you for making every shoot day feel like magic. And to the unflappable Francesca Crichton—we needed a Frankie in the house.

To Susie Theodorou, who is amazing at making food look amazing, but also smart as hell, as honest as she is generous, and a brilliant f*cking cook. Thank you for taking me on.

To Lorenzo Music, whose spirit was with me when I sat down in front of a microphone for the very first time and realized I had something to say.

To Nina Lalli, ceramicist, sister, and retired prop stylist. You must have figured out by now that I needed you not only for the purple, pink, and green objects that made us both happy, but because you made me feel safe, grounded, and loved. I would have totally failed at this without you. Plus: Ruffles!

To Frank Lalli, my father and mentor, a man of inexhaustible determination, stubbornness, iron-clad work ethic, innate confidence, and questionable puns. Thank you for giving us a million great reasons to drink all of the wine.

To my mom, Carole Lalli, for being a bottomless source of information, advice, patience, and proper punctuation. But more importantly, for showing me what having a career, a family, and a life surrounded by true friends looks like, and for inspiring me to try to achieve at the same level.

To Leo, my savory breakfast eater and fearless cook, thank you for being my most honest recipe taster, and for loving kimchi as much as I do. And to Cosmo, for teaching me that a person can really love food without necessarily liking every food, and that we should all just eat more of the things we like.

But most of all to my Fernando, for being the single greatest support, source of love, and anchor in my life. Our being together made it possible for me to do a big thing on my own. I cannot imagine going through this time on earth without you as my partner in all things, and I wouldn't want to, either.

Index

A

Aioli and All the Things for
  Dipping, 126–27
Almond(s)
  Charred Broccoli Salad, 107
  Cinnamon Spice and Honey Is
    Nice Brittle, 260
  Praline Meringues, 258–59
Anchovy(ies)
  Cream, Spring Lettuces with, 84
  Spaghetti Aglio e Olio with
    All-o the Parsley, 143
Appliances, 26
Artichoke Hearts, Quick-Braised,
  Spaghetti with, 136–37
Asparagus
  Grilled, with Smoky-Spicy
    Brown-Butter Bread
    Crumbs, 111
  sautéing, 40–41

B

Bacon
  Carbonara Stracciatella, 131
  -Fat Fried Eggs, BLTs with, 118
  Mushrooms, and Kimchi, Fried
    Grains with, 125
  and Peanuts, Stir-Fried Celery
    with, 104
Basil
  Caprese Mac and Cheese, 144
  Mayo, Paprika Plancha Shrimp
    with, 188
  Pesto, Clams, and Corn, Fregola
    with, 148
Beans. See also Green Beans
  Fox-Style Chickpeas, 233
  Grilled Squid Salad with
    Cucumbers, Herbs, and
    Smoky Chickpeas, 192
  Pasta e Fagiole, 224–25
  and Slow-Roasted Lamb
    Shoulder with Magic Green
    Sauce, 216–17
Beef
  Butter-Basted Rib Eye with
    Crunchy Fennel Salad,
    200–201
  Grilled Short Ribs with Serrano-
    Cilantro Marinade, 208

Pork and Brisket Bollito Misto,
  210–11
Ribs, Slow-Roast, with Melted
  Peppers and Horseradish,
  204–5
Beets
  30-Minute Spatchcock Chicken
    and Vegetables, 164
  Buttery, and Grapefruit, 92
Black Bass, Crispy-Skinned, with
  Salt-and-Butter Radishes, 184
Blenders, 26
Boiling and simmering, 57–61
Bread Croutons, Garlic, Chicories
  with, 95
Bread Crumbs
  Big, Cauliflower, and Sausage,
    Pasta with, 140
  Smoky-Spicy Brown-Butter,
    Grilled Asparagus with, 111
Brittle, Cinnamon Spice and
  Honey Is Nice, 260
Broccoli, Charred, Salad, 107

C

Cabbage
  Pork and Brisket Bollito Misto,
    210–11
  Stir-Fried Celery with Peanuts
    and Bacon, 104
Carbonara Stracciatella, 131
Cardamom seeds, 27
Carrots
  Pork and Brisket Bollito Misto,
    210–11
  steaming, 52–53
  Yogi's Kitchari with Sizzled
    Spices, 234
Cauliflower
  Pan-Roasted Salmon with
    Cauli-Tartar Sauce and Chive
    Vinaigrette, 187
  Sausage, and Big Bread
    Crumbs, Pasta with, 140
Cayenne, 27
Celery, Stir-Fried, with Peanuts
  and Bacon, 104
Cheese
  Caprese Mac and, 144
  Carbonara Stracciatella, 131

Charred Broccoli Salad, 107
Fresh Figs with Manchego and
  Wet Walnuts, 96
Greek-ish Grain Salad, 151
Ham-and-Butter Baguette with
  Green Beans, 103
Mozzarella with Charred and
  Raw Sugar Snap Peas, 87
Omelet with Whipped Ricotta
  for Two, 121
Seared Lamb Patty with
  Marinated Halloumi and
  Herbs, 221
Chicken
  Cutlets with Spicy Coconut
    Dressing, 167
  Rack Roasted, with Gravy
    Potatoes, 163
  Rosemary, Ragu with Pressure
    Cooker Polenta, 170–71
  Spatchcock, and Vegetables,
    30-Minute, 164
  Thighs, Pan-Fried, with Italian
    Salsa, 168
  Wings, Spice-Drawer, 175
Chickpeas
  Fox-Style, 233
  Smoky, Cucumbers, and Herbs,
    Grilled Squid Salad with, 192
Chicories with Garlic Bread
  Croutons, 95
Chocolate and Vanilla Mousse,
  263
Cilantro-Serrano Marinade,
  Grilled Short Ribs with, 208
Cinnamon Spice and Honey Is
  Nice Brittle, 260
Cinnamon sticks, 27
Clams
  Buttery Pan, with Ginger,
    Scallions, and Grilled Bread,
    191
  Corn, and Basil Pesto, Fregola
    with, 148
Coconut
  Coconutty Collards Slaw, 100
  Dressing, Spicy, Chicken
    Cutlets with, 167
  No-Stir Maple Granola, 156
Coffee Crème Caramel, 246–47

Collards Slaw, Coconutty, 100
Compote, Fruit, with Labneh, Maple Syrup, and Olive Oil, 244
Confit, Duck, My Way, 176–77
Confit method, 63–67
Coriander seeds, 29
Corn
    Clams, and Basil Pesto, Fregola with, 148
    Fresh, and Corn Broth with Popcorn Spices, 237
Cornmeal Cream Shortcake-Biscuits, Mom's, 255
Crème Caramel, Coffee, 246–47
Croutons, Garlic Bread, Chicories with, 95
Crushed red pepper, 29
Cucumbers
    Herbs, and Smoky Chickpeas, Grilled Squid Salad with, 192
    Salted, with Ginger and Chile, 99
Cumin, 29

D

Duck Confit, My Way, 176–77

E

Egg(s)
    Aioli and All the Things for Dipping, 126–27
    Bacon-Fat Fried, BLTs with, 118
    Carbonara Stracciatella, 131
    Dozen- , Slow-Cooked Frittata, 117
    Fried Grains with Bacon, Mushrooms, and Kimchi, 125
    Omelet with Whipped Ricotta for Two, 121
    Poached, and Silky Braised Greens, 122

F

Farro
    Fried Grains with Bacon, Mushrooms, and Kimchi, 125
    Greek-ish Grain Salad, 151
Fennel Salad, Crunchy, Butter-Basted Rib Eye with, 200–201
Fennel seeds, 29

Figs, Fresh, with Manchego and Wet Walnuts, 96
Fish. *See* Seafood
Food processors, 26
Freekeh, in Pomegranate-Parsley Tabbouleh, 155
Frittata, Slow-Cooked Dozen-Egg, 117
Fruit. *See also specific fruits*
    Any- , Galette, 242–43
    Compote with Labneh, Maple Syrup, and Olive Oil, 244
    Mom's Cornmeal Cream Shortcake-Biscuits, 255

G

Galette, Any-Fruit, 242–43
Garlic
    Bread Croutons, Chicories with, 95
    granulated, 29
    Spaghetti Aglio e Olio with All-o the Parsley, 143
Ginger
    and Chile, Salted Cucumbers with, 99
    Scallions, and Grilled Bread, Butter Pan Clams with, 191
Grains. *See also* Oats
    boiling and simmering, 58–59
    Fried, with Bacon, Mushrooms, and Kimchi, 125
    Pomegranate-Parsley Tabbouleh, 155
    and Roasted Squash with Spicy Buttermilk Dressing, 152
    Salad, Greek-ish, 151
    Yogi's Kitchari with Sizzled Spices, 234
Granola, No-Stir Maple, 156
Grapefruit and Buttery Beets, 92
Green Beans
    Green-estrone, 228–29
    Ham-and-Butter Baguette with, 103
    Pan-Fried Chicken Thighs with Italian Salsa, 168
Greens. *See also* Lettuce(s)
    Chicories with Garlic Bread Croutons, 95

Coconutty Collards Slaw, 100
Pasta e Fagiole, 224–25
Silky Braised, and Poached Egg, 122
Slow-Cooked Dozen-Egg Frittata, 117

H

Ham
    -and-Butter Baguette with Green Beans, 103
    Pasta e Fagiole, 224–25
Hazelnuts
    Brown Butter, and Chives, Seared Scallops with, 183
    Pan-Roasted Romanesco with Toasted Nuts and Crispy Bits, 91
Herbs. *See also specific herbs*
    Grilled Short Ribs with Serrano-Cilantro Marinade, 208
    Herbaceous Grilled Lamb Chops, 214
    and Marinated Halloumi, Seared Lamb Patty with, 221
    Slow-Roasted Lamb Shoulder and Beans with Magic Green Sauce, 216–17
Honey and Cinnamon Spice Is Nice Brittle, 260

K

Kale
    Pasta e Fagiole, 224–25
    Slow-Cooked Dozen-Egg Frittata, 117
Kimchi, Bacon, and Mushrooms, Fried Grains with, 125
Kitchen organization, 23–26
Kosher salt, 30

L

Labneh, Maple Syrup, and Olive Oil, Fruit Compote with, 244
Lamb
    Chops, Grilled, Herbaceous, 214
    Patty, Seared, with Marinated Halloumi and Herbs, 221

Lamb (*continued*)

Shoulder, Slow-Roasted, and Beans with Magic Green Sauce, 216–17

Leeks

confit, preparing, 64–65

with Potato Chips and Chives, 108

Lettuce(s)

BLTs with Bacon-Fat Fried Eggs, 118

Carbonara Stracciatella, 131

Chicken Cutlets with Spicy Coconut Dressing, 167

Greek-ish Grain Salad, 151

Spring, with Anchovy Cream, 84

Lobster Pasta with Grated Tomato Sauce, 146

M

Maple

No-Stir Granola, 156

Syrup, Labneh, and Olive Oil, Fruit Compote with, 244

Meat. *See also* Beef; Lamb; Pork

slow-roasting, 70–71

Melon Salad, Savory Summer, 88

Meringues, Praline, 258–59

Mousse, Chocolate and Vanilla, 263

MSG, 30

Mushrooms, Bacon, and Kimchi, Fried Grains with, 125

Mustard seeds, 30

N

Nuts. *See also* Almond(s); Hazelnuts

Cinnamon Spice and Honey Is Nice Brittle, 260

Fresh Figs with Manchego and Wet Walnuts, 96

No-Stir Maple Granola, 156

Stir-Fried Celery with Peanuts and Bacon, 104

O

Oats

Cosmo's Power Pancakes, 159

No-Stir Maple Granola, 156

Omelet with Whipped Ricotta for Two, 121

P

Pancakes

Cosmo's Power, 159

Swedish, Birthday-Worthy, 252–53

Pan-roasting, 45–49

Paprika, smoked, 30

Paprika Plancha Shrimp with Basil Mayo, 188

Parsley

All-o the, Spaghetti Aglio e Olio with, 143

-Pomegranate Tabbouleh, 155

Pasta

all'Amatriciana with Confit Tomatoes, 135

Caprese Mac and Cheese, 144

with Cauliflower, Sausage, and Big Bread Crumbs, 140

e Fagiole, 224–25

Fregola with Clams, Corn, and Basil Pesto, 148

Green-estrone, 228–29

Lobster, with Grated Tomato Sauce, 146

Spaghetti Aglio e Olio with All-o the Parsley, 143

Spaghetti with Quick-Braised Artichoke Hearts, 136–37

Pastry Dough

preparing, 75–79

10-Minute, 241

Peanuts

and Bacon, Stir-Fried Celery with, 104

Cinnamon Spice and Honey is Nice Brittle, 260

Pea(s)

Green-estrone, 228–29

Snap, and Scallion Salsa, Pork Steaks with, 197

Sugar Snap, Charred and Raw, Mozzarella with, 87

Pepper, freshly ground, 30

Peppers

Grilled Short Ribs with Serrano-Cilantro Marinade, 208

Melted, and Horseradish, Slow-Roast Beef Ribs with, 204–5

Salted Cucumbers with Ginger and Chile, 99

Pesto, Basil, Clams, and Corn, Fregola with, 148

Pimentón de la Vera, 30

Polenta, Pressure Cooker, Rosemary Chicken Ragu with, 170–71

Pomegranate-Parsley Tabbouleh, 155

Pork. *See also* Bacon; Ham

and Brisket Bollito Misto, 210–11

Pasta with Cauliflower, Sausage, and Big Bread Crumbs, 140

Ribs, Glazed and Charred St. Louis, 198

Steaks with Snap Pea and Scallion Salsa, 197

Potato Chips and Chives, Leeks with, 108

Potato(es)

Gravy, Rack-Roasted Chicken with, 163

Green-estrone, 228–29

Pork and Brisket Bollito Misto, 210–11

Sweet, with Tahini Butter, 112

Pots and pans, 26

Praline Meringues, 258–59

Pressure cooker recipes

Glazed and Charred St. Louis Pork Ribs, 198

Rosemary Chicken Ragu with Pressure Cooker Polenta, 170–71

R

Radishes, Salt-and-Butter, Crispy-Skinned Black Bass with, 184

Rice

Fried Grains with Bacon, Mushrooms, and Kimchi, 125

Yogi's Kitchari with Sizzled Spices, 234

Romanesco, Pan-Roasted, with
Toasted Nuts and Crispy
Bits, 91
Rosemary Chicken Ragu with
Pressure Cooker Polenta,
170–71

S

Salads
Charred Broccoli, 107
Chicories with Garlic Bread
Croutons, 95
Greek-ish Grain, 151
Grilled Squid, with Cucumbers,
Herbs, and Smoky Chickpeas,
192
Melon, Savory Summer, 88
Pomegranate-Parsley
Tabbouleh, 155
Salted Cucumbers with Ginger
and Chile, 99
Spring Lettuces with Anchovy
Cream, 84
Salmon
Aioli and All the Things for
Dipping, 126–27
Pan-Roasted, with Cauli-Tartar
Sauce and Chive Vinaigrette,
187
Salt, kosher, 30
Salt, sea, 29
Salt and Pepper Cooking (SPC),
about, 34
Sandwiches
BLTs with Bacon-Fat Fried
Eggs, 118
Ham-and-Butter Baguette with
Green Beans, 103
Sausage, Cauliflower, and Big
Bread Crumbs, Pasta with,
140
Sautéing, 39–43
Scallion(s)
Ginger, and Grilled Bread,
Butter Pan Clams with, 191
and Snap Pea Salsa, Pork
Steaks with, 197
Scallops, Seared, with Brown
Butter, Hazelnuts, and Chives,
183

Seafood. *See also* Anchovy(ies)
Aioli and All the Things for
Dipping, 126–27
Buttery Pan Clams with Ginger,
Scallions, and Grilled Bread,
191
Crispy-Skinned Black Bass
with Salt-and-Butter
Radishes, 184
Fregola with Clams, Corn, and
Basil Pesto, 148
Grilled Squid Salad with
Cucumbers, Herbs, and
Smoky Chickpeas, 192
Lobster Pasta with Grated
Tomato Sauce, 146
Pan-Roasted Salmon with
Cauli-Tartar Sauce and Chive
Vinaigrette, 187
Paprika Plancha Shrimp with
Basil Mayo, 188
Seared Scallops with Brown
Butter, Hazelnuts, and
Chives, 183
Sea salt, 29
Seeds
Cinnamon Spice and Honey Is
Nice Brittle, 260
No-Stir Maple Granola, 156
Shellfish. *See* Seafood
Shopping strategies, 21–22
Shortcake-Biscuits, Mom's
Cornmeal Cream, 255
Shrimp, Paprika Plancha, with
Basil Mayo, 188
Slaw, Coconutty Collards, 100
Slow-roasting, 69–73
Smoked paprika, 30
Soups
Carbonara Stracciatella, 131
Fresh Corn and Corn Broth with
Popcorn Spices, 237
Green-estrone, 228–29
Pasta e Fagiole, 224–25
Yogi's Kitchari with Sizzled
Spices, 234
Spices, essential, 27–30
Squash
butternut, pan-roasting,
46–47

Roasted, and Grains with Spicy
Buttermilk Dressing, 152
Slow-Cooked Dozen-Egg
Frittata, 117
Squid, Grilled, Salad with
Cucumbers, Herbs, and
Smoky Chickpeas, 192
Steaming, 51–55
Swedish Pancakes, Birthday-
Worthy, 252–53
Sweet Potatoes with Tahini
Butter, 112

T

Tabbouleh, Pomegranate-
Parsley, 155
Tahini Butter, Sweet Potatoes
with, 112
Toaster ovens, 26
Tomato(es)
BLTs with Bacon-Fat Fried
Eggs, 118
Caprese Mac and Cheese, 144
Confit, Pasta all'Amatriciana
with, 135
Pan-Fried Chicken Thighs with
Italian Salsa, 168
Sauce, Grated, Lobster Pasta
with, 146

V

Vanilla and Chocolate Mousse,
263
Vegetables. *See also specific
vegetables*
Aioli and All the Things for
Dipping, 126–27

W

Walnuts, Wet, and Manchego,
Fresh Figs with, 96
Wheat berries
Fried Grains with Bacon,
Mushrooms, and Kimchi, 125
Grains and Roasted Squash
with Spicy Buttermilk
Dressing, 152

Published in the United States by Clarkson Potter/
Publishers, an imprint of the Crown Publishing
Group, a division of Penguin Random House LLC,
New York.
crownpublishing.com
clarksonpotter.com

CLARKSON POTTER is a trademark and POTTER
with colophon is a registered trademark of Penguin
Random House LLC.

Library of Congress Cataloging-in-Publication Data
Names: Music, Carla Lalli, author.
Title: Where cooking begins /
    Carla Lalli Music.
Description: First edition. | New York: Clarkson
    Potter/Publishers, 2019.
Identifiers: LCCN 2018024658 | ISBN
    9780525573340 | ISBN 9780525573357 (ebook)
Subjects: LCSH: Cooking. | LCGFT: Cookbooks.
Classification: LCC TX714 .M8728 2019
    DDC 641.5—dc23 LC record available at https://
    lccn.loc.gov/2018024658

ISBN 978-0-525-57334-0
Ebook ISBN 978-0-525-57335-7

Printed in China

Book and cover design by Decade
Photographs by Gentl and Hyers
Food styling by Susie Theodorou
Prop styling by Nina Lalli

10 9 8 7 6 5 4 3 2 1

First Edition